Youtube Marketing

Use Marketing Strategies for Make Money Online With Youtube

(Learn the Video Content Marketing Secrets and How to Start a Youtube Channel for Business)

Garry Irwin

Published By **Phil Dawson**

Garry Irwin

All Rights Reserved

Youtube Marketing: Use Marketing Strategies for Make Money Online With Youtube (Learn the Video Content Marketing Secrets and How to Start a Youtube Channel for Business)

ISBN 978-1-77485-931-5

All rights reserved. No part of this guide may be reproduced in any form without permission in writing from the publisher except in the case of brief quotations embodied in critical articles or reviews.

Legal & Disclaimer

The information contained in this book is not designed to replace or take the place of any form of medicine or professional medical advice. The information in this book has been provided for educational and entertainment purposes only.

The information contained in this book has been compiled from sources deemed reliable, and it is accurate to the best of the Author's knowledge; however, the Author cannot guarantee its accuracy and validity and cannot be held liable for any errors or omissions. Changes are periodically made to this book. You must consult your doctor or get professional medical advice before using any of the suggested remedies, techniques, or information in this book.

Upon using the information contained in this book, you agree to hold harmless the Author from and against any damages, costs, and expenses, including any legal fees potentially resulting from the application of any of the information provided by this guide. This disclaimer applies to any damages or injury caused by the use and application, whether directly or indirectly, of any advice or information presented, whether for breach of contract, tort, negligence, personal injury, criminal intent, or under any other cause of action.

You agree to accept all risks of using the information presented inside this book. You need to consult a professional medical practitioner in order to ensure you are both able and healthy enough to participate in this program.

Table Of Contents

Chapter 1: Youtube Is One The Most Powerful Search Engines On The Planet... 1

Chapter 2: Quickstart To Setup Your Channel.. 7

Chapter 3: 10 Fundamental Steps To Create A Perfect Youtube Channel.......... 21

Chapter 4: 6 Fake Beliefs Concerning Youtube Seo... 27

Chapter 5: Unrealistic Expectations 32

Chapter 6: Tips, Tricks & The Ultimate Stratges For Keywords. Titles. Subtitles. Tags. Thumbnails. Descriptions.............. 37

Chapter 7: 7 Steps To Improve Your Youtube Channel's Success Immediately 46

Chapter 8: Tip & Tricks To Grow Vertically Your Youtube Channel Audience And Attract More Buyers 63

Chapter 9: 9 Secrets To Reach Big Numbers When You Are A Prominent Creator Of Contents On Youtube 79

Chapter 10: 19 Ideas That Will Make You Money With Youtube 99

Chapter 11: Understanding Youtube Promoted Videos 116

Chapter 12: How To Get Youtube Monetization Started 133

Chapter 13: Youtube's Algorithm Operates 163

Chapter 14: How To Market On Youtube: An Introduction 183

Chapter 1: Youtube Is One The Most Powerful Search Engines On The Planet

YouTube is undoubtedly the most popular website online for video creation, but it's also number three. Many people don't take advantage of all the social networking benefits it provides. YouTube users rarely use the platform to establish a brand or build their online presence. Many YouTube users have never even uploaded one video. YouTube should be viewed as a serious consideration if you're new to the concept. Here are some reasons.

* Cross Promotion - YouTube is a great tool for cross-promotion. YouTube can be used to direct viewers to your blogs or other websites. After your videos are over, tell viewers where to find you on your blog. Don't forget reminding them to subscribe. YouTube can be used on its own. But YouTube is only as useful as a complement to other blogs or websites. You must promote your channel on a regular schedule.

* A Full-Time Income is Possible: This is possible. Some people have made full time incomes through YouTube alone, especially with the AdSense program Google offers. However, it is important that you have multiple income streams in place when you start. AdSense may not offer as much income as other strategies, but that doesn't mean you should ignore it.

* Grow your business by having videos on YouTube. Your content is more popular than other types of content. The more content they see, the more they will keep it watching. They will also be more likely to subscribe to your content and visit your other websites. You don't need to have more content, but you do need quality!

Now you are more aware of the reasons for bringing your advertising and advertisement efforts to YouTube. Market directly to your target audience through video format. You can also connect via comments and channels. YouTube has many sharing options that are similar to what you would find on any website or social media. YouTube users can share videos on Facebook, Twitter or email. This function is great for customers who love to share their achievements about a company with just a click. This is how you can make it easy to share the success of your company.

YouTube now supports "real-time upgrade" YouTube now has a feature called "real-time updates." This allows companies to go social and create a link between YouTube and customers. YouTube's Insight Statistics & Data on Line Films are another very useful feature for entrepreneurs. This allows you keep an eye on the number and quality of the views that your picture receives. It also shows the achievement rate of your picture's message via ratings. You're right! It's completely cost-free.

YouTube: A Short History

YouTube's rich history is captivating. Jawed Karma, Jawed Karim and Steve Chen were all former PayPal employees when the Web site was launched in February 2005 as a web hosting site. The partners had left their previous company to start a new venture. After trying many different ideas, they realized the need for a tool which allowed downloading, viewing and sharing video. YouTube was thus born.

The couple licensed YouTube.com's domain on February 15, 2005. After that, they began working in Hurley's workshop to create the web technology. Chen, the programer of the bunch, worked with Adobe Flash's Flash's development language to stream videos within a web-browser. Hurley, an expert user interface designer, introduced the tag idea. It allows users to post and define the videos that they like. Together, they developed a way that users could post video clips on their website. This increased site's functionality. In December 2005, the company was officially founded after Sequoia Funding, Menlo Park (California) raised venture capital. YouTube became a major player in the market almost immediately after its launch. In the first month of operation, YouTube had three million visitors. This is quite impressive for a startup. The site saw a triple increase in visitors after February (to 3 million), but again this was tripled by July (30 million), and the site had 38 million visitors at the end.

YouTube became one of the world's top 10 websites, making it one of history's most-visited websites.

This type of growth wasn't unnoticed, mostly through rival websites. Google, the largest rival platform, was determined to purchase the company. It did this in October 2006. YouTube was paid $1.65B by Google - an incredible amount for such young companies and one that has to make significant sales.

YouTube is located right at the center of Google's enormous empire. YouTube operates independent from Google, so YouTube's platform continues to work as before Google. YouTube acts and looks the same today, just like it did before Google. The only difference is distance. YouTube continues to exist today as an autonomous entity. Wikipedia reports that YouTube's bandwidth investment is close to $1,000,000 per day, despite Google having large pockets. That amount is comparable to other figures.

YouTube wasn't first to offer online content access, but it was an excellent timing.

BusinessWeek was told by Steve Chen, co-founder, that YouTube's success is due to several factors.

* The advent and affordability of video cameras.

* Extension of fiber lines in 1999 and 2004

* YouTube's growth has been remarkable despite the fact YouTube did not properly monetize its content.

YouTube viewers can comment on pictures. Marketing's purpose is to connect with viewers in a way which brings people and products together. Online people aren't afraid to share their thoughts. When people comment about movies, entrepreneurs are able to get honest responses from viewers and receive tips for making new ones.

Chapter 2: Quickstart To Setup Your Channel

YouTube has many video tutorials and in-depth guides on how to create a YouTube channel. But I will show you some of the essential steps and give you some insider tips to make your channel more successful.

Let's set up your channel correctly to ensure that YouTube Gods smile down on us.

These are the four things you must do before you start your channel.

* The right mindset

* The right channel names

* The best strategy

* YouTube Journal (or any notes app on your phone), but I recommend getting a note-taking notebook and pen.

The Right Mindset

In other words, you have to clearly define the purpose of your channel and be confident in what you can provide. Don't try to do everything. This will limit your potential growth and hinder your chances of success. YouTube can only be successful if you identify and develop your talent. It is easy for you to create content on many different topics, which can lead to a lack of interest in your audience. It is likely that you will end up wasting your time and not being able to reach the first 1000 subscribers.

The long-view is also an important aspect. YouTube is not for you if you seek instant gratification. YouTube will not allow you to get rich quickly. Nothing good can be built in a single day. It's now time to start preparing yourself for the next two.

The Right Name for Your YouTube Channel

Your channel name is very important because people will associate it with your name. Names should be meaningful, readable, memorable and easily remembered. The shorter the title is, the better. When you build a YouTube brand, ensure the name you choose matches the rest. You should create a sense of coherence if you have both a website as well as other social media channels. I encourage my clients to use their name, or choose a name that conveys the core message.

Writing down words that best reflect you and your goals for this channel is a great way of getting your creative juices going when name-searching. The words you use to describe the type content that you are publishing will help you think of ideas. If you are targeting a specific audience, it is a good idea to add words that reflect your personality. Then play with the words to see if you can come up with something.

Spinxo, a tool to help you find the perfect name for your channel and give you some ideas, can be used as a source of inspiration.

The Right Strategy

Your YouTube channel should be managed strategically. If you don't, it will fly blind.

One of the reasons I was stuck with my channel was because I wasn't executing a growth plan. So nothing was going to change. All athletes know that they must arrive at the game well prepared. Otherwise, they won't be able compete with the rest of the field. You can think of this moment as your preparation before you go into the game. Your success rate will be half that of those who didn't know better if you learn more strategies and tactics.

It was said so well by a friend, who is also a YouTube beauty influencer. She stated that she had to work seven years to reach 50,000 subscribers. In just one year, she was able to go from 50K viewers to 300K. She did this not because unicorns were magically sprinkled on her channel. But because she carefully planned out and implemented a strategy.

I want you to have a strategy before you begin to "wing it".

Make Your YouTube Channel

Step One: Sign up for a Google account.

You can sign in by going to Google or YouTube. You'll be prompted to sign into your existing Gmail accounts. Otherwise, just follow the screen instructions to sign up for new Gmail accounts. You will find a "settings" cog icon in the upper left corner of your screen once you've signed-up. Click to create your channel.

Step Two: Create Your YouTube Channel.

This includes choosing the channel icon, channel artwork, channel description, and so on. You will also be asked whether you would like to create your channel using a company name, a personal or another name. The instructions vary depending on whether this is a product, brand or company.

Once you have created the channel and signed in, you can click on your user icon to open the channel menu. For further customization, you can navigate to the channel, switch accounts and return to your dashboard.

Step 3: Provide additional information such as links, contact details, and a trailer.

My suggestion is to add links on your YouTube channel in order to help your audience access other marketing avenues. This is a fantastic tip if your website or social media platforms have you interested in driving traffic to. YouTube allows users to control how many links are displayed on their channel art. In the "About", section of your channel, I recommend that you include your contact details. This makes it easier for people who have seen your value to inquire about you. Even though most people forget about the channel trailer, I found it very influential in attracting new viewers. The channel trailers play automatically whenever someone visits your channel. It's an excellent way to grab their attention, show them who you are, and let them know what value they can expect. You need to be thoughtful about what you post here. Keep it brief, to-the-point and memorable.

Insider tip

Your dashboard will contain the community link, where you can respond to, delete, or flag comments as spam. By going to your creator studio, you can view the comments. So that others feel connected to you every time you upload a new video, I encourage everyone to reply to every comment.

You can also change the community settings. If needed, you can add moderators to review comments. Also, comments that contain links or hashtags should be held for review so that they don't go public. It is important to regularly review chat messages, especially those that are posted during Live stream.

Step Four: Upload the first video.

Before you publish the first piece that will take you to the top, be sure to read the privacy statement. This will help you avoid having your channel taken down. There are a few privacy settings that you can use when publishing videos. The video can either be public (anyone can view it), anonymous (only the person who has the link can see it), private or scheduled (release it on an agreed date in the near future). I recommend starting with "Private" so you don't make mistakes or upload the wrong video. Once you feel you are ready, you can switch the video settings back to public.

The last thing you need to keep in mind is that each video must be optimized to maximize its success. This includes thumbnails and titles, descriptions, tags, and tags. Let's discuss each one a bit further.

Thumbnails

Because this is what viewers see first, customizing your thumbnails is a smart idea. Do not get too obsessed about it. Just put in the time. Customizing thumbnails will give your channel a cohesive look and professional feel. If you type in your keywords, this can help you stand out in a YouTube Search.

Tags

Keywords in YouTube Land are keywords. The phrases or questions people type in the search box should be core to your video optimization. YouTube is a search engine. It is easier for your video to appear on their feeds if you include the keywords your ideal audience is typing in the tags. Long-tail keywords work best, but ensure that the words you use are relevant to the search terms. Google will penalize you for not attracting people in order to get views. To add multiple keywords to the search, simply type your phrase in "Tags", then hit enter or add a space.

Title

You only have seventy characters to convey your compelling message. Make sure you are as brief and clear as possible when describing the content of your video. This will help people to understand what to expect. Your video title should offer potential viewers an appealing reason to click through. This doesn't mean you should use clickbait titles and misleading information. It should be consistent with the thumbnail picture you created.

A thumbnail with Beyonce's image and a video title that says "my shocking Interview with Bey" is not acceptable unless you did actually interview her. Beyonce has been open about reviewing and discussing things in her thumbnail. Make sure the thumbnail is precise and appropriate.

Description

You should also include a description of what your video covers. YouTube's search system and discovery system use video descriptions. YouTube's algorithm relies on video descriptions as a key source of information. The copy here should be relevant to the reader.

Also, it should include the main phrases and keywords that were used in the Tags field. This area can also be used to add links to your website or other calls to action.

Think mobile

Keep in mind that most people view mobile sites via their smartphones. You want potential followers to notice your image and read the words. Consider adding words to your thumbnail. Mobile users will view the image at a smaller size so that you can convey your main message.

These are just a few of the crucial things that you must do to set up your channel. Let's now discuss the essential equipment needed to become a YouTube sensation.

Are you looking for expensive and complicated equipment?

Absolutely not. You can see the YouTubers have amazing studio setups, with lots of lights, different camera angles, as well as what appears to an army of professionals supporting them in producing TV-quality videos. It shouldn't cause you to lose your cool. To be honest, I don't think anyone has the time or need for all that. I will share with you the things you need, regardless of your budget.

The only YouTube Equipment Checklist You Need, With or Without a Price

We live at the best time in human History, when each person can carry a mini studio and broadcast their content for free. That's right. You can always spend money to make your equipment fancier, professional-looking, and higher quality, but don't let any of that stop you if you're starting the business with zero funds.

For those with zero budget

All you need is to get started building real followers, making YouTube money, and living the life you've always wanted is:

1. Smartphone.

2. Camtasia (free for Mac) and iMovie (free).

3. Canva, a graphics editing software for creating thumbnails is available for free.

4. A large window to allow the sun to enter through.

5. You'll need to have some books and an echo-free space so your audio will be clear and your image won't be shakey.

These three pieces of tech and the free sun are all you really need.

For those with a smaller budget

You can invest as little or as much as your heart desires. I can promise you that any investment you make will bring in high dividends. For example, in the last two years I have invested around $2,000 into equipment and software for YouTube. I've earned over $45,000 just in ads. I've also sold thousands of sponsorships and affiliate products.

As you can see the initial investment proved to be very lucrative. You must remember, though, that I did not start with the equipment. It is up to you to choose what equipment and when. In any case, I'm going share the material and tips with you that I wish had been there when I first started.

These are some tips to improve the professionalism of your channel and increase your video views.

1. A quality camera that can capture high-quality video.

I recommend the Canon 70D DSLR. This camera is capable of continuous shooting for 30 minutes and is extremely easy to use, even for beginners.

2. High-quality lapel microphones.

It doesn't necessarily have to be very expensive. Lav or Lavalier mics are my recommendation. They pick up background noise better than camera-mounted microphones. It is actually very affordable and produces excellent sound. YouTube viewers might allow poor lighting to go unnoticed, but you must have excellent audio quality or else they will all disappear. Amazon's Rode and Blue Yeti brands are worth checking out. They offer great sound quality at a very reasonable price. Additionally, you can buy a microphone that plugs into your Camera or smartphone.

There's One More Thing

This is the best advice that I can offer (especially over the long term), and I'll leave it at the end.

Learn to do SEO (search engine optimization)

YouTube is second in search engine traffic. SEO is the practice of getting to the top of search results, especially for those with large volumes.

It is important to remember that we are talking of permanent traffic that is completely free and that it can be reached in huge volumes depending on which niches (specific search terms).

Chapter 3: 10 Fundamental Steps To Create A Perfect Youtube Channel.

YouTube allows you to create channels themes that include fashion, literature or music. Every day, YouTube posts new videos in short formats. They are often uploaded without any production.

This format has many views and loyal fans, which makes it attractive to advertisers and YouTube. The fun of creating videos can also be a business.

At first glance, setting up your own YouTube channel might seem intimidating. But it is possible to imagine that there are many things you need to consider in order for your channel become a success. Do not be discouraged. This is possible by taking care to the essential details and being organized at each step. Find out what they are.

Step 1

Talk about your likes

It makes you feel more comfortable being on camera. A cooking channel is a great option if you're a skilled cook.

Step 2

Missing the mark of creativity

YouTube hosts many different types of channels. Once you've chosen your theme, get creative and start creating something new. There must be a difference if you want your channel to stand out from the crowd.

Step 3

Let Your Ideas Be Printed

To develop any subject, you can use the following methods: Create a script, take notes, draw topics, and then remember them.

"You don't have the obligation to repeat every word you plan. This would be something very rehearsed. It's important to have a solid base for recording so that you don't get lost.

Step 4

Your commitment to updating the Channel

Begin your vlog with a day in the week. Next, plan to get the video posted to YouTube. The journalist states that "not only do people need to know when news will be available, but also in order to gain YouTube space and establish their channel,"

Then, you can increase the amount of vlogs. This includes frames and replying tags. These are very common YouTuber activities. Make sure you keep your promises to your viewers!

Step 5

Keep an Eye On All Network

YouTube allows for lots of interaction in comments. YouTube also calculates your number subscribers. Subscribers receive email notifications whenever new videos are added to the channel. However, there are still people who use Instagram, Twitter, and Facebook to receive notifications about new videos.

YouTube expert and YouTuber, Alexis Smith, said that he had learned the importance networks from his own experience. He stated: "I always notice a rise in views whenever there is an Instagram video or other networks.

Step 6

Listen to Your Audience

Once you have the main subject of your channel, it will make it easier to draw the interest public. The internet is flexible. It allows us all to create new things. YouTube is one of the most popular platforms. A channel can be used to create new boards or invent.

Step 7

Be confident in your personality

YouTubers should not be ashamed to show their true self. Consider using your best and lightest feature to make videos. You can be the joke in your group, so show your funny profile. Do not be afraid to tell people that you are normal.

Step 8

Choose the Best Scenario

It is essential to choose a quiet location where recording will not be disrupted. You will need to set up this place at least once you start your vlog. If there is sufficient lighting, consider decorating with fun items. You might find it embarrassing to record on a white background.

Step 9

Use what you have to do

You don't have to spend thousands on professional equipment such as microphones, lighting and cameras. Instead, you can consider how your channel will grow and what the needs are.

To begin with, a camera with good resolution in a well-selected location is essential.

Step 10

Editing is essential for a successful business.

If you don't know what to do, it is a good idea for someone to guide you. Editing vlogs requires the ability to remove long lines. YouTube content is more engaging than television. YouTube viewers prefer to watch short videos. Editing allows you to adjust the length and/or make long videos more interesting. Editing videos can be used to add soundtracks and animations. This will help you identify your channel.

Chapter 4: 6 Fake Beliefs Concerning Youtube Seo

Many people have preconceived views about YouTube. Let's get rid of some myths we may have believed in the past.

Fake belief #1

YouTube Success is only possible if you are viral

YouTube success is most often discussed by people who are video bloggers and have millions of viewers. Some of their viral hits helped them rise to fame.

Naturally, we tend only to pay attention to the rare exceptions and assume that being viral is the only way of making it big on YouTube. This simply isn't true.

It is essential to master YouTube ranking. Ranking videos refers to getting videos on search results pages in the top position. The more it is "ranked", you'll get more clicks and views, as most people don't scroll beyond the first pages.

If you generate a lot of traffic for free and build your subscriber base quickly, you can be very successful.

You don't have to depend on luck. There is a proven system which works, provided you put the effort in to implement it.

Fake Belief #2

YouTube can make you money if you have millions of views or hundreds of thousands.

YouTube Ads are the most popular way YouTubers make money. You need to get a lot more views to make a decent amount of this revenue stream.

YouTube makes money, but you don't have to get that many views. All you need is a good video, a call to action that makes a point, and a product your audience loves.

Important: Calls-to-action are clear directives that you add to your video's end or middle. They direct the viewer to sign up, comment, like, click the link or follow the description.

You can then start selling.

Even if only 50 views per video are received and you only make one sale each day, you could still make hundreds of bucks per month with this video. It is something that I have done.

Fake Belief #3

YouTube SEO Hasn't Worked Since A Few Years

It was simpler to just "stuff" your meta fields with the exact keyword to rank for.

SEO experts frequently refer to these terms. There are three terms that SEO experts frequently refer to: "Blackhat", Whitehat, or "Greyhat".

Blackhat techniques are those that do not comply with the terms of service for any platform they're being used. These are spammy tactics that try to use the system to gain an unfair advantage over natural searches results.

Whitehat techniques are those that adhere to and are consistent with the guidelines and best practices of any platform where they are being used. These require more work but are very sustainable over the long-term.

Greyhat tactics can be described as those that are somewhere in between Blackhat and Whitehat. They strive to appear natural while still taking advantage parts of the platform to gain an edge.

YouTube (and Google) have become smarter, more advanced and can now use 'keyword-stuffing' as a blackhat tactic. But, proper whitehat YouTube optimization techniques are effective. These techniques look natural, organic, give YouTube more context, meaning, and help YouTube understand what your video's about.

Fake Belief #4

Viewers Only Want to See Humorous Videos

YouTube is not for everyone. Not everyone wants to see funny YouTube videos. Many people visit YouTube to search "howto" videos, view inspirational or motivational clips, and hundreds of other reasons.

YouTube videos that are most popular include product reviews, vlogs. gaming, comedy, shopping.

Fake Belief #5

Your videos should be of Hollywood quality to be successful

Absolutely not. The most important aspect of content is video quality. Modern smartphone cameras are capable of creating high quality videos with excellent video quality.

Do you recall watching a movie with incredible special effects that was completely lacking in content? This is evidence that video quality does not matter. The content (or the story) makes the film great or terrible.

Fake Belief #6

Promoting videos can be expensive

It doesn't cost anything to promote your videos. Learning how to rank your videos will save you a lot of money on paid advertising.

You just have to be innovative and think outside the box.

Chapter 5: Unrealistic Expectations

It doesn't matter how many times you fail, because eventually you will master it. This can lead to you losing your way. If you are like others you may give in to temptation and stop working towards your goals.

YouTube is where you want to make money. Learning from other people's mistakes will help you. This will cut down the time it takes to make YouTube money.

#1 Fatal Error

Unrealistic Expectations

YouTube stars have high hopes for their success. They believe that a quality video will make it popular and bring in a lot money.

You can also adopt this mindset by slowing down. Your work doesn't end once your video is uploaded. Uploading your video only marks the beginning a new stage that will require even more work. In particular, you will need promotion for your video. Even then, don't assume you will make money instantly. It takes time.

Fatal Mistake #2

Focusing too much on short videos

You will only be able to tell the difference between a video that is valuable and a video that is not. Your videos may be shorter as you are still learning the ropes. However, these videos usually don't cut it.

They do not provide enough information for viewers to assist them. A one-minute review isn't enough to make a solid assessment of your brand new phone. Search engines prefer longer videos to be displayed in search results. Google searches for "how do you draw a cartoon character?" returned results that are more than 3 minutes.

This does not mean you need to include fluff to make the video last longer. Viewers won't be patient and will not finish the video. YouTube uses the percentage that was viewed to measure quality.

Buffer Social research found that the ideal length of a video is 2 minutes 54 seconds. You shouldn't let that stop you from having fun. It is possible to create a video that lasts longer than 3 min if you have compelling reasons. I've seen videos as long as an hour and still managed to get many views.

Fatal Mistake #3

Neglecting Audio Quality

Many people can handle a poor video. However, only a few people can endure bad audio. We may think of the image as more important than audio, which can make it seem confusing. The truth is that audio matters too.

A stand-alone microphone is essential, as I have said before. This will make your camcorder sound better than its built-in mic.

Recording must be done in a quiet space. To eliminate the outside noises, close the doors and windows. To reduce the sound of popping, you might also consider using a pop filter.

If it's impossible to record audio at the same time as the video is being shot, start with the footage and do the audio last.

Fatal Mistake #4

Being everything

Without a main theme, no one will want to subscribe your channel. It might be that you have videos related to fashion, music, sports, or tech products.

Instead, create a channel to cover every niche. This will make it easier for you to reach your target market.

#5 Fatal Mistake

Selling too much

While advertisements can be enjoyable to watch, they still have the potential to make viewers miserable. Viewers don't want to watch endless advertisements.

It is your choice to sell as much or as little as you wish, but it is best to strike a balance between giving and selling. Selling too little will make it difficult to earn the loyalty of your customers. This will enable you to make more money.

Fatal Mistake #6

Too Much Editing

Excessive editing can make your video look amateurish. It is essential to shoot great videos. This will make it easier to cut out unnecessary editing.

YouTubers with a passion for YouTube are not to be stopped by the mouse. These YouTubers add so many effects to videos that it is difficult to watch them.

One rule that you must remember is: editing videos only if you understand what you are doing will enhance them.

Chapter 6: Tips, Tricks & The Ultimate Stratges For Keywords. Titles. Subtitles. Tags. Thumbnails. Descriptions.

#1 Channel Keywords

A YouTube channel well-designed will help search engines recognize your videos a lot better. As a result optimization will improve both your YouTube rating and your rank in search engines like Google. Metadata is very important to YouTube, and channel keywords are an important component of that. These are one-to-two-word descriptions of your channel which allow users to get a feel for what your content is all about. They can be added from the Creator Studio advanced settings to your YouTube account. But net keywords can only be used in a proper way to improve ranking. Do your research about the keywords relevant to you and your company before you start using them. Google AdWords Keyword Planner (or Rank Monitor) are two good tools to help with this.

#2 Video Title

YouTube videos have the same importance as blog posts, and SEO is equally important. YouTube videos also have metadata which is an important rating factor. This includes the description of your video. Search engines, Twitter, and consumers have the first view of your video's title. A well-titled video can draw more viewers and boost views. The best titles are shorter, since longer titles can be broken up depending on the search engine, app, and application. With that in mind, try to keep video titles to five to fewer terms. Your title should include keywords at the beginning. Keywords should always be relevant and pertinent to the particular video.

#3 Video Description

YouTube views the video description as well as the title as the most important rating criteria. YouTube and Google cannot extract information about your picture. A text explanation will help determine the quality your video. If you don't include one, search engines may not be able to determine what your video's content is. Your rankings may suffer. Your video description should contain at least 250 words, and the keywords that are relevant to it.

To increase your SEO benefits, include your keyword within the description's first 25 characters. You can also link to external URLs (e.g., your social media channels, related blog content) for additional SEO benefits.

#4 Image Tags

YouTube can use tags to provide additional insight into the quality and context of your image. Tags are not as important as the description and title of your video but they can still impact how it ranks. Tags can be used to help users find the content they are looking for. Keywords can be described as tags. Think about the possible phrases people might use to search for your picture. Tags such as "optimizing website posts" and "SEO on web" could be used to describe your video.

You should remember the keywords you used for the rest your site. Be sure to use appropriate tags and don't go too far. Ten well-researched relevant tags is better than twenty unrelated ones.

#5 Quality in Video

Video quality is an important consideration when rating. So, HD images have higher ratings than those with low resolution. YouTube's search results prominently highlight HD videos. The user experience is greatly affected by video quality. For example, a low-quality clip that has top-notch content can potentially lead viewers elsewhere. YouTube cannot do this. Google and Bing use backlinks, and other cues, to determine the content's quality. You need to evaluate quality content. It should place emphasis on user interaction. A low user engagement sends a clear message to YouTube's crawlers. Simply put, even if you have great SEO, your videos won't rank high if they aren't of HD quality.

#6 User-Experience Measures

YouTube rates videos based on user engagement. YouTube also uses multiple user-experience measures to evaluate the quality.

YouTube doesn't use backlinks. Instead, it uses user engagement data like comments, subscriptions after viewing and shares to help determine consistency. YouTube will rank a video with more engagement than a low quality picture. YouTube is also able to see if a video has attracted viewers from your site. It sends a signal that the video contains an exceptional piece of material. The content retention measure is another key user experience measurement. It is the number of people who watch your content. YouTube will notice if there is no interest in a 5-minute video. This indicates that YouTube is unhappy with the video.

The basic idea is that YouTube will know if someone likes the video and wants to view it full-screen, leave a comment or subscribe. The easiest way to get feedback is to ask your audience a question during the show. Another way to get more interaction is to encourage fans to subscribe, and then to thumbs down the video.

#7 Live Time

YouTube uses "watchtime" (or what it calls it) since late 2012 to determine the accuracy and usability of its videos. The length of each display time is what YouTube refers to as "watch time". YouTube used to rely on views only before its creation. This ensured that videos could still get high rankings, even if they had high bounce rates. YouTube was a tool that could be used to manipulate or even commit violence, such as buying videos. It didn't provide any indication of quality or pertinence. YouTube today places a great deal of value on watching time. The algorithm prioritizes videos which results in an average watching experience that lasts longer than shows that receive more. You can use the YouTube Analytics views report and the Audience Retention report to determine which channels have highest and lowest viewing rates. This will allow you to plan the next content accordingly. A great way to increase the time a user spends watching videos is to use notes to leave connections to other videos within the description field.

#8 View Count

YouTube does not place much emphasis on how long you spend watching YouTube videos. However, YouTube views are an important factor in rating YouTube. More views are equal to higher rankings-particularly for competitive keywords. It is clear that if you want your videos to rank well for more competitive keywords you must get lots of views. It is essential that you take steps to promote your video content to other sites. This can increase your videos' visibility, and your views will go up. This is a simple way to make your images more visible in blog posts. They can also be posted on social media platforms and blogs like Quora to raise impressions.

#9 Thumbnails

Thumbnails have an important effect on click through speeds. Choosing the right thumbnail will increase your views and your rating. YouTube will automatically generate thumbnails from a screen shot of your film. However, videos with custom thumbnails still perform better than those that use automatically created images.

It is important to take the time to create a thumbnail for each one of your images and then upload it. It should be appealing to the eye and draw attention. It should be appropriate to the contents of the video. Thumbnails with a resolution 1280x720 px and an aspect rate of 16:9 are generally more effective.

#10 Closed Captions, & Subtitles

YouTube allows you attach captions to videos. This includes spoken-word material. However, many publishers overlook closed captions which can be a serious mistake. Two reasons closed captions are helpful for rankings include: It exposes the content and makes it more accessible to a wider audience, including those who can't hear or speak another language than the one being used in the picture. This raises the score and counts. Search engines may crawl close captions. This can provide a significant boost to your ranking.

YouTube does have automated captioning. Although it is not perfect, some changes might be needed. Alternately, you can upload the captions. Analysis YouTube has a lot of content uploaded every minute. It can be difficult for your videos to rank well and stand out on YouTube.

Chapter 7: 7 Steps To Improve Your Youtube Channel's Success Immediately

These tips on uploading will ensure that you don't miss the chance to improve your YouTube video before it goes live.

Although uploading videos to YouTube may seem simple, you are missing out on the most effective ways to make your channel popular.

Other than being able to tell the world's second-largest search engines what your video is about; the upload process gives you an opportunity to engage viewers and get them doing exactly what it is that you want.

YouTube allows you to upload most video formats like MOV (movie), MOV (avi), WMV, FLV and WMV. You can convert to mp4 using Handbrake (free conversion software).

Larger video files may take more time to upload and then process. Uploading an mp4 file that is 15 minutes long can take up to half an hour. While the upload is taking place, it is important to keep the browser tab open. But you can also open other internet tabs while waiting.

We will be discussing four main elements of the upload screen in separate sections.

After uploading your video, there are options to add closed captioning cards or an endscreen.

Practical Step 1.

Closed captioning your YouTube videos

Closed captioning for YouTube videos is very important. About one in twenty people have hearing loss. Captions will allow you and your community to reach this audience. You can also use captioning to distract from the noise at work. Closed captioning is used in about 8% to 9% of my viewers.

Closed captions also help YouTube to identify the content of your video and rank it in search. The platform makes its own captions but doesn't trust these enough for search discovery.

You can easily caption your videos by using a teleprompter to script your videos. All you need is the text you want to copy and paste into the captions area.

1. Click Subtitles/CC on the video information screen.

2. Click to add new subtitles and choose the language.

3. Choose Transcribe, or auto-sync.

4. You can either paste your text or create captions.

5. YouTube will take at least an hour to sync text and audio. Click back to review the captions and then approve them.

Rev is also available for hire to transcribe your videos. This service is charged at a dollar per min, which can make it expensive for new creators.

We will be discussing scripting and using an teleprompter throughout this book. This is another of the many benefits. There is a learning curve in creating a prompted clip that looks natural. I don't think I have it all figured out yet. However, the pros outweigh the disadvantages. It is easy to add captions and read from the prompter to edit videos.

Practical Step #2

Add End Screens for Your YouTube Videos

It is easy to add end screens in YouTube videos.

An end screen shows the last 10-20 seconds of video. This is where you can encourage viewers to view more videos or add your subscribe call. YouTube makes this simple by displaying end screen elements at fixed positions on the screen.

Use one of the YouTube templates to create an endscreen. Simply click Use Template. The screen will display a range of formats, including video boxes or a subscription prompt, at various points.

When you know which template your vIdeo will use, you can add text callouts pointing at the elements to your video. An example: I ask people to click the arrow pointing towards the image, just above my Subscribe element on my endscreen template.

You can ask viewers to watch your recent upload, select video or playlist, or let YouTube choose the best video for them based on their history.

* I always choose the most recent upload for the first video element displayed. This is a way to get as much traffic as you can to your newest videos to give it that watch-time boost in those first two days.

* YouTube trusted me to know my viewers better and I would select Best For Viewer for the next video element. Instead, I switched to adding playlists because they typically translate into higher watch-time per viewer.

It's crucial that you are talking through your screen and providing content. Viewers will lose focus if the informational section of the video is finished. They'll also be more likely to be distracted by other content or suggested videos. Instead, make sure they are focused on your video and prompt them to click through to the end screen.

You can alter the timing of your final screen elements for up to 20 seconds.

Practical Step #3

Scheduling YouTube Videos

I have talked to creators with hundreds of thousands of subscribers who publish their videos within minutes of uploading. They may have a particular day and time that they want to publish each week, but they wait until last minute to get their videos published.

To me, that sounds exhausting. And one unanticipated delay can make them disappoint their community.

While it can be difficult to schedule video production weeks in advance, it is easy to keep your videos on the right track. You will never be late if you publish the same number videos each week.

This is how it would look: If Seinfeld had no episode for Must See Thursday, what kind of happy would NBC be?

A professional channel is one that has a video ready for each day, optimally several days per week. It is essential to plan at least a few weeks in advance so that you have enough time to schedule your videos.

Uploading a YouTube video will quickly become a routine. The process is so straightforward that it's easy to mindlessly zoom through the video.

Resist the temptation

Research the metadata and points beneath your videos as much as you spend on creating them. For every video, do it and you will see amazing growth.

Practical Step #4

Video Metadata to YouTube Success

Although the upload process is not difficult in some cases, like uploading the description or tags, they aren't as important. You have a great opportunity to get your videos out there.

This opportunity centers on metadata...sorry.

Metadata refers to data (information) that describes another data. Metadata, in this instance, is information that describes the contents of your video.

YouTube is not a person. YouTube won't be able to watch your video, and then say, "OK.

This video is about paying down debt." I'll rank them with these videos regarding debt." YouTube and Google are both experts in understanding content. YouTube can help you guide it in the right direction, but it is still up to you.

It's clear that metadata on a YouTube video (especially the titles, tags and descriptions) is even more important the first week. YouTube doesn't have any data on viewers reactions so it uses metadata from your video to quickly rank it within the relevant topics.

You can create a video that sounds natural by knowing the keywords you'll target in your video.

*Remember to include metadata in your YouTube videos. It is important to think about whether you want to modify the metadata after a video has been published. You also should not change metadata that is already performing well.

YouTube tracks the performance of your video based on how many views it receives and how long it takes to watch for keywords. This is how YouTube ranks your video for search and recommended videos. YouTube must now learn what metadata the video has and if it changes the metadata, everything is reset.

It doesn't mean that you shouldn't modify metadata after a published video. If it has been six months since the last video was published, then you may want to refocus the keywords and rewrite the description to give it new life.

Practical Step #5

How to Select Your YouTube Video Tags

Old school bloggers will always remember when an article could be stuffed with keywords in order to rank higher on Google. Bloggers would include keywords in a list within a paragraph. This was to help them rank.

YouTube was also the first platform to allow you to do this.

This is not the case, either fortunately or unfortunately depending on how your eyes look at it. While the importance of the tag field for your video upload has diminished, it is still crucial to do the necessary research to find the best tags.

A new channel cannot rank for the most relevant keywords. You can tag keywords in your descriptions all you like, but you are unlikely to be in the top 20 for a keyword as competitive as 'making money online'.

Instead, go deeper into niche ideas such "making money for teenagers" and "making money as an adult". It is better for a video to be ranked in the top 5 for a less-used keyword than being buried in 50th place for one with high-traffic.

Keyword research can be done starting with a core topic or a popular idea based upon a high-traffic keywords. You then move on to more niche ideas. This will allow you to find smaller keywords for your description tags. You can also build a content strategy by creating individual videos about each keyword.

Smaller channels (less than 25K subscribers) should focus on keywords that rank between

100 and 1000 searches on YouTube. For monthly traffic statistics, you can use Keywords Everywhere Chrome extension.

Start by typing your core topic idea into search to see what YouTube auto-populated for niche ideas

Use the alphabet-search option to search for your core topic keyword. Then, type the keyword in search and then go through the alphabet. Add each letter to the end to see what ideas you get.

Ideally, you will want to use between 10-15 niche keywords related your video. These keywords will be used both in the video description and in the tag field. These will be used in your video description and tag field.

There are 500 characters you can use in your tag field. That could be a lot of keywords phrases. While you don't necessarily need all that space, I suggest using 10 to 15 tags. YouTube will recognize your video's keywords by using three or four keywords.

Practical Step #6

Making a viral video title

I loathe thumbnails and titles! I find it frustrating that you can't simply create a beautiful video and expect viewers to see it. If you want people to click through to view your amazing video, then it is imperative that you have a captivating title and a persuasive thumbnail.

It can be frustrating but that is how it works. Spend the time for each thumbnail and title, and you'll find it worthwhile.

The art of creating a great title takes only two steps. Even if you don't consider yourself artistically gifted, that's a good thing.

Let's start with some basic points. Next, I will share a free tool to help you with this process:

Your main keyword or phrase should be included in the title. Google search does not consider this as crucial, but YouTube search shows that titles with the keyword in the title are more effective than those without it.

Three types are better than the others: lists (how-to), questions, and questions.

Although characters should not exceed 70 characters in length, data suggests that titles with 50 to 60 characters perform better.

To seperate a part of the title, you can use [] brackets.

Use words that trigger emotions such as fear, anxiety and happiness. Examples include words like surprise, frightening, blissful and terrifying.

Use words that stimulate curiosity such as "you won't believe it" or "you'll be astonished".

Your best title isn't about inspiration. It's about brainstorming. It involves spending at most 15 minutes brainstorming different ideas, then searching Google to find the best ones.

The headline analyzer is not a perfect tool, but it's useful to test different ideas and determine which gets a higher score. Your intuition is a good tool to help you choose the title.

Practical Step #7

How to Create Your YouTube Video Description

I'm shocked at how little time creators invest in video descriptions. Even the largest channels will often only include a handful of links in their description.

Your video description is a tremendous opportunity on many levels and something that should never be ignored.

YouTube will use your description to determine how and where to rank the videos. This description also gives you an opportunity to make more money, retain viewers for longer periods of time, and convert subscribers.

You can put up to 5,000 words in your video description. This is roughly 800 words. But you don't have to use it all. I aim to use 300 words to describe the video. After that, I will add a template section which contains subscribe links and additional content. It is approximately 150 words.

These are some suggestions for things to include in your description

Your video's description should be keyword-rich (duh). Use keywords from your tags research to make your video convincing. Talk about what content you'll share and why the viewer should see it. You should at most write a few hundred words.

A Table of Contents could be added to your description. It would list the time that each main point is mentioned in the video (Example: 1:53). This will encourage people to watch the video instead of clicking away, and it also allows you to include keyword-rich topics.

Call out relevant videos and add links to them. This is an excellent way to keep viewers on your YouTube channel.

You should include a couple of affiliate links. Don't include too many affiliate links and only one that is directly related.

A callout in one or two sentences describing why someone should subscribe. Then, add your subscription link.

Make sure to reach out to any link magnets that might be of interest to an email list.

YouTube is only a machine. YouTube is a machine that needs YOU (the user) to help understand what a particular video is all about by using metadata. YouTube Needs Your Help!

YouTube will rank the first few lines of your description for search. These are given extra weight and increased visibility by YouTube.

Please note: Links that lead people away from YouTube. YouTube doesn't like when you take people off its site. YouTube viewers can click off your videos to hurt your search rankings, while YouTube viewers stay on the platform after you've posted them.

You shouldn't include a link that links off-YouTube. Earning money from affiliate links or adding people to an email list are both good reasons. Video content should be relevant for affiliate links.

While it's entirely up to you to decide what you put in your video description. I have seen some strange stuff that you might not want to include.

* A clickable long list of video equipment. Do your viewers really care about it? Are the pennies you earn on Amazon worth hurting your video if they send them off to YouTube?

* Random affiliates not related to the videos. YouTube will see the off-site link even though viewers aren't clicking it. This may be worse than helping.

* Too many social networking links. This one is difficult to argue. If you want to attract viewers to YouTube, then you should try to build a network on other platforms.

Chapter 8: Tip & Tricks To Grow Vertically Your Youtube Channel Audience And Attract More Buyers

It is essential to have a successful YouTube channel in order to stand out from others who are trying to achieve the exact same success you desire.

It is possible to surpass anyone who is trying to reach your target market if they approach you with the right intent, attention, desire, and determination. All you need is a greater desire to connect with your audience and more consistency.

Create the Perfect YouTube Page

It's very easy to put together a YouTube Channel. You can learn a lot from the website, and you'll be an expert in no time.

The About Section.

YouTube profiles don't pay enough attention to the About section. This is a common mistake. This is due to the fact that when you view someone's profile, it's usually hidden in another tab instead of right at front. In contrast to most other social media networks, which are right at front.

Although the character limit is not as strict as some others, it should be short, sweet and simple. Keep it simple and limit the number of characters you use. You can say what you believe, your message, or your goals. You don't have to use hashtags.

Include links to any other social media pages or websites in your description. YouTube allows up 5 links. You can even personalize hyperlinks up to 30 words. Consider putting your email address in business, just in case others want to get in touch with you.

Your Cover and Profile Photo

Keep your profile image as well as your cover photo simple. For your profile photo, use your logo. If you want to use your logo as your cover picture, choose a large image that includes your slogan or a brief description of who and what you are. A good rule of thumb is to keep things simple, at the very least, for the first few times. You should make it visually appealing.

Your YouTube Trailer

YouTube gives you the ability to choose which video to display at the top of your webpage. A trailer, clips, and other elements can be put together to showcase the content of your channel. You can just keep doing your best work, especially when you're just getting started. Your first video to potential customers should be your absolute best, best-respected video.

High-Quality Video Content

These are some great tips for creating YouTube videos.

#1 Make sure to use a lot of lighting

Video should be bright.

#2 Use a Clear Background

Filming on messy or chaotic backgrounds (unless it's intentionally) will result in a low-quality video that makes you look unprofessional.

#3 Use a Clear audio

Audio quality is as important as video quality. A poor-quality video is more popular than bad audio.

#4 Avoid having shaky feet

It gives the impression that someone was sick or that you have an obsolete device. You can use a tripod to stabilize your movements if you shake too often.

#5 Improve Your Camera Presence

Distractions can be caused by being nervous, uneasy and fidgety. You want to appear competent and knowledgeable.

#6 Uploading Your Videos

Uploading videos to YouTube can be done in minutes.

On the YouTube main webpage, look for an upwards-pointing pointer arrow. Click on this arrow for the upload page. From here, you can select any video file you've previously edited.

Once your video is uploaded, you will be able to customize the headline and thumbnail, description, as well the tags.

Click on your icon in top left corner of YouTube's main page to make further edits. A drop-down list will open. You will need to click Creator Studio. This is where all the tools are available to manage your YouTube account. You can access your "video managers" from the right-hand menu. From here, you can edit captions, modify the video, or make other changes to your video.

#7 Frequency's Importance

YouTube allows you to publish new content every day for your viewers. YouTube is a social networking website. Many people don't realize that YouTube favors accounts that share regularly.

YouTube will prioritize your content and rank you higher when people search for it. The more you upload to your YouTube channel, and the more friends and viewers engage with your videos.

You can think about any video-based service where episodes are shared often, such cable. The more content is consistently released, and the more people will tune to the content, the better. The first episode might get lots of hits but then it may start to fade away. But the consistent release of new episodes keeps people coming back.

As viewers return to the show to learn more, and become more captivated by it, the audience will continue growing. Your YouTube channel will experience the same thing. You might get lots of hits in the beginning, but you need to keep your frequency high. Content that you share will not be seen as often. YouTube success is dependent on your ability to keep it going and to increase its popularity. To do this, you will need to regularly upload videos.

Another huge benefit to posting new content regularly is that you drive new traffic back to your channel. Not only will you get new viewers, but your older videos will also be more visible. Your videos will be viewed by people who click on them. They may then go on to visit your channel to see other videos.

If you have many high-quality videos that are relevant and well-made, people will click through your older videos and see them. They will do more of this and rank your older videos higher. Your overall growth rate will also increase exponentially.

#8 Create a Consistent Intro and Outro

The consistency of your YouTube channel content is an important consideration. It is possible to create consistency by keeping the core message and approach the exact same. But, you can increase that consistency further by adding short intros or outro clips that introduce and summarize your videos.

This is similar to the intro and theme music of your favorite television shows. Each episode ends with a short credits' sequence. This will help you easily recall all your favorite episodes.

It is likely that you remember the Friends theme tune, even though it has been used many times and played on TV for so long. This consistency can be replicated in your videos by creating short intros with music and other information that introduce your viewers.

You don't need much more than a basic intro, but it is important to remain consistent and easy to identify online. So that your clips aren't subject to copyright infringements you must ensure that the music is free from royalty. Select some high-quality images and a brief intro film to the music. Once you are done, add words to introduce your channel, the episode, or perhaps your usernames on other social media platforms.

Your intro should be under 25 seconds. This will help you to convey consistency without going overboard. You may find that your audience clicks to "similar" videos for the same information if you have too many clips. This could lead to your audience clicking to a video with the exact same information.

#9 Post Your Content on Multiple Networks to Advertise Properly

When you look at YouTube's most lucrative YouTube stars, you will see that their descriptions of videos link to their social networks.

This is a great way to cross-post for even more engagement. This is also an organic way to promote your brand. You can get more engagement from your followers and build loyalty to your brand by cross-posting the links.

Once you upload your videos, share them with all the social media pages. You can cross-promote among your YouTube channels. YouTube offers a variety of advertising options so you can promote your content to other channels that are relevant and relateable.

#10 Monetize

If your new videos receive at least 1,000 views each video, you will know that your subscriber base is sufficient to enable you to begin monetizing your page beyond affiliate links. The monetization tab, which is the key to this is built into your channel.

This tab can found in your options menu. YouTube will place relevant advertisements prior to your videos. It's also important to connect your channel and Google AdSense. In turn, this will turn on ads based on each viewer's browser history.

Both of these types advertising will begin with a pay per Click structure. However, if your subscribers reach sufficient people you will eventually be able access to pay per View advertisements.

You should not use copied material in your videos if you are looking to make money this way. Pay per click typically pays 20 cents per person. That's because 1,000 views is sufficient to assume that 10 people will click on your advertisement. If you are able to build enough followers to be eligible to receive pay per click ads, you can make approximately $3 for every 1,000 views of the ad.

#11 Become A YouTube Partner

While this last step is critical to maximize this potential affiliate revenue stream, it's not something that you can do alone. All you can do is keep creating quality content. Once your videos have reached a certain number of regular viewers, you'll receive a letter.

After you have done this, affiliate links can be placed directly in your videos and not just in your description. This means that you will want to make sure you have a short link description. Nobody is going to click on a URL if it takes up more than three lines.

Affiliate Marketing

It is also a good idea to sign up for an affiliate marketing program, such as Amazon Associates.

You must be careful when you start to work as an Affiliate Marketer. Don't go too crazy with the sales pitch. This is a sure way to lose all those viewers you worked hard to acquire.

It's a better idea not to make videos but to introduce a new segment every other week in which you review products that you think are of interest to your niche. This will ensure that your viewers receive useful content as well as a positive reputation for you.

Depending upon your content marketing strategy and goals, reviewing products relevant to your niche is often one the best ways of bringing in new members of target audience. A product review can easily bypass the sales pitch defenses that so many people make. The review contains almost all of what a pitch should contain without adding any stigma. While a review may help customers avoid spending money on a bad product, a sales page can be seen as a pushy advertisement.

You should be as open as you can about the strengths and weaknesses of a product when writing product reviews. If you review a product without making it clear and justifying your recommendation, especially when you're first starting affiliate marketing, then readers will be less likely to trust you with products.

Your YouTube page is part your brand, so you should protect it no matter how high the commission per sale may be. It is important that your reviews include personal experiences with the product, including photos. Your readers need to be able place themselves in your shoes.

Although the pay-per sale commission model can be a great way to make big incomes as a vlogger, it is only possible for those who sell the right products. Your job as an affiliate marketer is limited to convincing your readers to click the link. Once they have clicked, the seller must complete the sale. You should ensure that the seller is honoring the deal when you are advertising products.

The best way to conduct product reviews is to concentrate on one product or group of product with a very critical eye. This means you'll need to be able to identify the weak points of the product, or product line, and then focus on its strengths. The illusion will be destroyed if this type of content is not as objective as possible. You should include both positive and negative reviews in your review to make it easy for your audience to judge your integrity. These reviews can be written with two to three links that will allow the reader to buy the product.

Broad Strokes Reviews.

Depending on what products are most relevant for your target audience, an in-depth product review may be too difficult to film. Focus on quick reviews, which typically only include a short shot of the product. Then you will need to summarize the product's key points and add a rating. These reviews are most effective for products with low prices, which viewers simply want to learn about before making a decision.

These types of reviews have a higher click-through rate than other types. Users are more likely, with the aim of finding more information about the product, to click the link. These posts may include a summary of similar products, as well as a ranking from the best to the worst. This is because your target audience is more likely than others to watch just one video describing 10 products. Additionally, only one video per product will be seen by more people. A single video is more effective and more appealing.

Comparisons.

A comparison piece can be an excellent way to show that a product you have a strong interest in is superior to others in the same market. Simply compare the strengths of each product along with any feature parity. The stronger product will then speak for itself.

A comparison video can be a great way for you to share your feelings about a particular product. This review can be expanded to include other products, and if done properly it will bring you a lot of traffic.

Negative Slant Reviews.

Negative slant review are different to outright negative ones. A review with a negative bias is meant to convince people who are naturally contrarian by adding caveats to the review that are sure hook them and draw in them.

You should therefore focus on the positive attributes of the product to create content. Then, don't be afraid to criticize the product for being too complicated or expensive. This will only make it more suitable for those who are most passionate about the topic.

If you do it right, many people will be willing or able to prove your wrong.

Chapter 9: 9 Secrets To Reach Big Numbers When You Are A Prominent Creator Of Contents On Youtube

Secret #1

Get Traffic to Facebook

Go to a fan site where you might find potential customers.

Let's say that you are reviewing a shaving cream. Next, you look for people interested in shaving.

It is important to start a conversation with others.

Once you've established contact with the person, you can give them suggestions about how to shave more effectively, what to use for shaving cream, and how to choose an electric razor.

Post your video URL, and be sure to provide them with valuable content.

A Facebook group can be created for shavers. It is best to wait until your video has received at least a few hundred hits before you create a Facebook community for shavers. You want to make sure that the market exists before you decide to do this. This is entirely up to the individual. Some of my students started their Facebook fan pages and found it profitable.

Secret #2

Tutorial Videos (How To's)

These types of videos saw an increase of 70% in 2017 The 2017 increase was 70%. This implies that these videos have almost twice as many views than in 2017. Now you can see how much we expect it to grow in 2020.

These videos are my favourite. It's so easy to learn something by just watching another person do it.

YouTube can host tutorial videos if you are a pro at something or a skilled in it.

It's very easy to do. You can learn anything, from mathematics (a niche that is growing rapidly on YouTube) to interior decoration and beads making.

You can even create other types content such as compilations.

Secret #3

Title and Thumbnail. Let's Dig Deeper

It doesn't matter what video quality you have, if no one clicks it, it's useless.

It has been proven time and again that thumbnails as well as titles are two of the main reasons viewers consider watching videos from channels they do not already subscribe to.

The thumbnail is used to show a preview or your video, particularly if you are embedded on another site.

After creating a thumbnail for the video, you can upload it. Here's how it works:

1. Go to the "Video Manager"

2. Select the video to be edited and click "edit".

3. Select "Custom Thumbnail".

Tips & Tricks to Pick Your Thumbnail

1. You should include a thumbnail with a human face that expresses emotion to the subject.

Scientific research has shown that viewers are attracted to reactions such as excitement, sadness, joy, or sadness.

It is used by many YouTube stars, including scammers. It has made me a victim many times.

2. You must ensure that your videos have relevant pictures. Or else viewers will abandon you channel.

Your viewers want to see value in your channel. If they don't, it will drive them to subscribe.

3. Although the photo of a baby or a cute animal has the same effect as that of a toddler's, you should only use relevant photos.

4. Parts of the thumbnail have arrows and circles, one or both. This creates curiosity in viewers about what they are.

5. Bright colors are essential. Black and white are also possible, as they would be

distinguished from the stream of colorful thumbnails.

6. The title of your video should be informative and visually appealing. You should make your title catchy enough to capture viewers' attention and concise enough to be easy to read.

Your title should not be so long it could be cut from the display. You can make the magic pill a part of your title.

Here are some tips to help you get started:

a. Use superlatives, such as "top", or "best", whenever possible.

b. Keywords can be capitalized, but they shouldn't be used too much. It could become annoying for your viewers.

c. Use of the term "secret", stirs curiosity and has been scientifically proven increase participation.

d. Starting titles with the "Top X (an quantity) boosts viewers.

e. Use of "Versus [vs]". For example, Samsung Galaxy S8 vs iPhone X.

f) Shorter time frames for great tasks. e.g. A professional website can be built in 5 minutes.

g. Although you should be aware of the keywords I have already mentioned and use appropriate adjectives, you shouldn't make it too "over-the-top" to look like clickbait.

h. Look back at your YouTube history. Are you able to see patterns? You can see the titles of top YouTubers. If you think they are clickbait level 10, then yours should go up to level 8. Level 0 doesn't suffice, while level 10 is way too much.

Take a look at these examples:

Level 10: TOP 5 MEATY MEXICAN RECIPES 2019 BEST NEW RECIPES GONE WILD NSFW UNCENSORED.

Level 8 - Top 5 mouthwatering Mexican recipes that blow the Taco Bell out Of The Water

Secret #4

Promote your videos by using other social media platforms

This is one the best ways to grow your YouTube viewership.

It is important for you to realize that not all viewers will be part of the YouTube social network.

They are members of other social communities such as Facebook and Twitter, Instagram and many others.

YouTube is a great platform to promote your channel, but you will be missing out on many opportunities for viewers.

It's a great idea to join a Facebook page related to your niche and to post links about your videos there.

You should only upload one video at the time. Be patient and adhere to the group's rules. It's a great way for you to gain a lot of subscribers to your channel. It is important that you make yourself worth the attention of these

YouTubers. We'd be glad to talk more about this.

YOU CAN CREATE AN PROMOTIONAL FACEBOOK VIDEO, AND LINK IT TO A YOUTUBE VIDEO or CHANNEL.

Facebook prefers to you use Facebook live instead of sharing YouTube videos.

Secret #5

Learn from the Best-Performing Videos

Google Analytics will allow you to see the most popular videos.

Make sure to take time to review these videos and the promotional methods used. You can then use these for future videos.

Secret #6

Co-YouTubers and YouTubers: Promoting Your Channel

Collaboration could boost your channel's performance quickly, especially if the channels have a large subscriber pool!

It's like promoting sales for products to YouTubers who have many subscribers. Because of this, the advert will reach more people.

The same goes if your channel is popular and people refer to you channel. You will get more subscribers. YouTube descriptions were used for this purpose in the past. However, a new YouTube collaboration feature has been introduced...

This feature allows you assign credit to anyone who collaborates. Just enter the YouTube username and URL of their channel.

These steps can be followed to ensure a successful collaboration.

STEP 1. Check for compatibility

This factor will determine the success of a collaboration.

A channel that is completely opposed to the content of your channel or has nothing whatsoever to do with it may not be able for you to collaborate well.

If you have a channel that's dedicated to makeup and you wish to collaborate with a game channel or a cooking channel, this would be an example. In this case, you would be considered incompatible. But you may find a way together to complement each others' work. Compatibility goes beyond channel content. It also includes personality and character.

*STEP 2. Come up with an irresistible plan

An idea is the foundation for collaboration. It is important to have an idea of how you would like to collaborate.

If you don't have any idea, you won't be able to collaborate. And if you do have an idea, what are you going to say to the popular YouTuber with whom you collaborate? Here are some ideas to help you get started. You offer YouTubers a collaborative idea that will benefit both of them.

You are unlikely to find anyone willing to help you. This time, you aren't paying by money. Instead, you are investing in an idea.

It must be beneficial and useful for the person you plan to collaborate with. The collaborator should credit you for the idea. This will help you gain more subscribers. Both you and your collaborator will both benefit from it. Your ideas must be worth something to your colleague so that they would notice them and agree to your offer. Your goal should be to find a collaborator that is worthy of your efforts, but not too high.

If you're a small YouTuber, it is possible to approach people with ten times as many subscribers.

STEP 3 Make an offer

Most collaborations involve a prominent person collaborating with someone less well-known. Therefore, it is common that you will be the initiator.

Make an offer. Talk about how you plan on sharing the proceeds. You must make sure that all these plans are completed during your planning and idea generation stages before you can actually make the offer to your prospective collaborator. This shows your seriousness.

After the terms have been settled, you need to promote the collaboration. It attracts people's interest even before the actual collaboration. Promoting your video on social networks before it's released is one way to do this.

You could promote your release with hashtags. The hashtags allow you to connect multiple conversations within your video. The hashtags are used by big brands for promotion. So why not use them?

For instance, Heineken's hashtag is "open your world". To encourage your fans to use hashtags, add them to the title, description, video, and then use them as a YouTube Card.

It's important to get your collaborators and fans talking about the hashtag, encouraging more people to view your videos.

Secret #7

Finding Collaborators

These options can be used to search for collaborators in your video:

YouTube Community Forum.

YouTube partners with Google+

YTtalk forum.

Forum YTgamers

Tubebuddy community.

DamnLag.

Your chances of building a connection with potential collaborators are higher if you spend enough effort on these forums. If you live in close proximity to a well-known YouTuber, and have something you think could be useful for them, it's possible to start a partnership.

YouTube subscribers and views are important. You must be consistent.

This does not mean that you have to keep the same schedule every day. Although this creates anticipation in your viewers, consistency can also mean consistency with themes, personality, format and other aspects. These aspects are what keep people engaged. Your subscribers will be confused if you suddenly post videos that are not related.

Wait until your subscribers are happy to allow you to diversify. You can only add videos on topics that your subscribers approve of. You must satisfy them to retain them.

You can increase your audience by working with other YouTube creators.

It makes the video even more amazing for both subscribers and it also allows you to have better brainstorming sessions and produce higher quality content. It's win-win for both you and your subscribers.

A person with only a few views cannot work together.

It would be unfair to get only a few of theirs and all yours to theirs. You will need someone who is at least as good as you are or slightly better than you. But if they have a lot to offer and your viewer base is growing, you can collaborate with them.

You must agree to everything before you can work together. This will avoid any disagreements.

Secret #8

Advertise to make more money

YouTube allows publishers the ability to advertise on videos.

YouTube receives a percentage from the revenue generated by these ads.

To generate income, you can use the YouTube Partner Program.

Some users believe the publisher should revert back to the program, and start publishing ads after they've started their channel.

First, increase your audience and subscriber base on the quality of your content.

This will ensure they are there for the long haul.

You can also put ads in your advertisements without getting annoyed by your viewers.

They are more likely stay online to view the entire video including the ad.

The Partner Program is available to anyone who has generated a particular number of views on their videos within a specified time.

I will tell you this: It doesn't matter if the subscriber has purchased anything from the advertiser.

ALL YOU NEED IS TO PUT IN THE AD FIRST. THEN YOUR MONEY WILL BE GENERATED.

...You have the option to tie up with as few companies as you wish, depending on how many videos that you have available.

This is a simple way to sign up. The only thing you have to do to make transactions is to enter your bank account information or PayPal username.

YouTube is now the second-largest search engine online after Google. 30+ million users per day. Everywhere you look, there are people of all ages and educations who sit at home and make more money than lawyers, economists, or even CEOs.

Do you not agree?

Their Secret?

These people have the ability to create large audiences. It is all that you need to be an entrepreneur.

Remember that money is only available where there is visibility.

If you don't like the idea of spending $1000 to take a 26 week old Course...

I've got you covered. I'm going teach you how to grow your business / channel organically in 2020. This is cheap, and you don't need to spend a lot of cash.

This course will teach you how to increase your sales, leads and profit by contacting your subscribers.

Secret #9

Advanced Notions with Video Cameras

It is important to start with the idea of exposure. According to this definition, exposure is the amount or time at which light enters the sensor. Three parameters are essential to controlling the exposure.

1. ISO;

2. Opening the diaphragm

3. Shutter speed

Three Reasons Why You Shouldn't Leave Your Camera Automatically

Automatic mode can pose serious dangers to your camcorder. Learning is a time when you can trust the camera to make the right settings.

It's not perfect. Videography is more difficult than ever. The ISO setting could cause problems with the quality of your movie.

The following are the 3 main reasons not to do so:

1. The shutter speed could be incorrect

2. High ISO causes digital noise in images

3. You may experience exposure that changes during the shoot if you move.

Slowly learn to turn off the automatic mode, or one of the semiautomatic ones, and to set it manually.

Diaphragm Opening, Shallow Depth in Field

The diaphragm's opening will alter the depth of field. This is the part of the image that will be in focus relative the background.

Image Noise, ISO

If you've ever used an entry level video camera, then you'll have noticed that the ISO is increased in low light. This causes a distracting digital graininess which can cause the viewer to lose focus.

What is shutter speed and how does it impact filming?

This is a different situation than opening and ISO. You must be extra careful with how you set it. Fluidity can be affected, and shots may look less natural. Some videos, like static ones, can be adjusted to allow you to break with the 'standard values'.

Chapter 10: 19 Ideas That Will Make You Money With Youtube

YouTube can make you money, but it is important to know the details of your business strategy.

A clearly defined business model is the foundation of YouTube's YouTube channel. This will allow all video content and calls to action to be aligned toward that common goal.

YouTube can provide a lot of free traffic, but it's surprising how few YouTubers understand how to monetize that traffic.

The question you need to ask is: What are you going to do with this traffic? What is your final outcome?

It is to build an email database? Does it help you to increase your social network following on another platform or website? Is it to increase your blog's visibility and interaction? Is it to make more sales? It is to generate more sales? Or is it to help fill an event?

Ideas' List - Maybe you are unsure how you can make traffic work for you. Here are some options if you are unsure:

1. YouTube AdSense allows you to create funny and viral videos that can get 6- or 7-figure views.

2. Link to several landing pages, where visitors can enter their email to get a free download. This will help you build your email database. By giving value to them and occasionally offering products, you can build a rapport with them.

3. Review digital product software and link it to the product via your affiliate link.

4. Review Amazon products.

5. Get more product sales by driving traffic to the e-Commerce store.

6. Increase your Twitter, Facebook, Instagram and LinkedIn following to promote products or services on these platforms.

7. Ask them to join a Facebook VIP group. This will allow you to interact with them often, add

value, as well as get them on your marketing and email lists.

8. A/B split-test sales copy or optin pages so you can find the best version before you actually start paying for traffic.

9. For a decent residual income, sign them on to a $5-10/month Membership Site that will deliver them 10x more value then they are paying. After that, you can sell them on to a $97/month Program with even more value.

10. If you have an iOS/Android App, ask them to get it.

11. Get paid every time someone fills in a form, installs an app or triales a product by linking them to a CPA program.

Tools & Resources' Short List:

MaxBounty has a large selection of CPA deals.

PeerFly-This network also has a solid reputation and a variety of CPA offers to select from.

FlexOffers- A good CPA network to explore.

12. To generate leads for your niche business, drive your YouTube traffic directly to a landing page. Give something away in exchange for their emails. Later, sell the leads at premium prices.

13. You can "rent" the first line on your YouTube video description. This allows clients to put a link in that area for a flat monthly rate. In exchange, the client must pay you a flat fee monthly and then you should put the link that they provide in the first sentence of your description.

14. Clicks are sold to clients' websites via specific videos. Prices could range from $0.25 to $1.00+ perclick depending on how targeted the traffic was. First, shorten their link in bitly.com/goo.gl. Next, at the end the month, review the statistics to determine how many clicks it received. Finally, charge them based upon how many.

Tools & resources:

Bitly or Google.gl - These websites can be used to shorten URLs. You can also track how many people click your link. They each have excellent analytics dashboards and a QR Code Generator.

15. Create 6-12 video tutorials or video lessons and then create 36 to 120 additional videos that they may purchase as a product.

16. Invite them to join regular webinars in which you provide value. At the end, present them with a tempting offer of $500-$2,000.

17. Invite them to register at seminars or live events that are held in a certain location.

18. Interview experts in the niche you choose and give 25% for free on the channel. After that, you link to your site, offer them more interviews in return for email and then upsell the rest plus monthly for a membership fee.

19. Selling advertising spots on high-viewed videos can be done to companies or businesses similar in your niche. Calculate your cost by the second.

While this list doesn't cover all of the possibilities for YouTube traffic, I hope it gives you some ideas that will inspire you to create your own.

Take Action: First, pick one. Then, once you're confident with it, you can add another. Doing too many things at once will cause you to lose your focus and make it more difficult to track what's working.

Working with YouTube Influencers

YouTube offers the greatest ROI (return on investment) for influencer marketing on social media. Stars of these online videos are now more visible than mainstream celebrities.

YouTube stars are thriving because of their billion-plus audiences. What's more, the majority of the viewers are young people.

As most models have tried it, making a wish to market your products by linking to a YouTube influencer's following is a common and effective advertising strategy.

Advertising Campaigns - What are the Benefits of Paying Out

Influencers are more effective than an advertisement because the people who engage with a particular promoter or influencer have the potential to receive interaction from that person.

Brands can choose from a variety of powerful ways to reach their target audience.

You could include an influencer in an advert and place emphasis on their demographics.

Here are some facts that will help you to deal with YouTube Influencers.

Get started with Influencers. There are many platforms where you can find influencers. Here you will find information about the candidates, including price estimates and how to contact them. These are exactly the ways these platforms work.

How does a Partnership begin?

We can't deny that many brands focus on the influencer. You'll find many platforms which connect brands with vice- and influencers

Versa. Numerous people are more successful in securing brand deals than other individuals.

An example of this is when a brand seeks a Beauty Vlogger. Although you did not appear on Google's search result, that means you are not searchable. If you're not on the Google search result, it is likely that sponsorships won't be available to you. It is necessary to appear in the search result for any type of list.

What Does an Influencer Expect from a Brand in Order to Do their Job Well?

Aside from the millions of dollars an influencer can make, creative management is an important component. Brands must believe in the influencer's ability to connect with their audience.

Though brands can provide guidelines, they need to let the influencer create the idea for the video. Influencers spend hours listing and understanding their audience's tastes.

If the brand provides all information and then the influencer allows them to get it from the brand, the result is, a great influencing will be able come up innovative ways to advertise the product. The magic begins.

Will the Influencer be the right fit for the item being market?

You can learn more about the influencer and their audience by conducting research. Check out the comments and take a look at the movies. If the influencer has a lot to offer your product in videos, you will most likely choose him.

A YouTube Influencer Campaign that is Outstanding

An example: A YouTube influencer in the beauty tutorials field has five million followers and people are watching every move. If they were selling a new contour palette, these people would definitely buy it.

If a brand is willing to include an influencer in their campaign, they will be more likely to succeed. You don't have to give an influencer any restrictions or guidelines to make your campaign a success.

If the influencer does not want to manage the entire campaign, then simply share the relevant information with them.

How to monetize your videos the right way

YouTube allows you to monetize YouTube videos in many different ways. Google AdSense is the easiest method to make money. However, there are other ways to earn more.

Google AdSense

Google AdSense will be your main earning source if you are a YouTuber. Google AdSense allows you to publish ads through the search engine giant. Google AdSense allows content producers (website owners, YouTubers) to add ads on to their content. The number of clicks and impressions that ads generate for content publishers is what determines how much money they get.

YouTube Google AdSense Requirements

To be eligible to add Google AdSense directly to your YouTube channel, please apply to YouTube Partner Program. YouTube creators required at least 10,000 lifetime views in order to join the program. This was changed in January 2018

YouTube Partner Program now requires that creators have 4,000 hours watch time in the past year (12 month) and at least 1,000 subscribers. The monetization option in your channel and account will not appear until you have met these view-and subscriber requirements. You can start making videos and growing your viewership if you're starting a new channel. Then, slowly but surely, you will reach these requirements.

YouTube will also check that your account remains active. This means you must avoid posting any content that is not allowed on the YouTube platform. This includes content with copyrighted material, excessive violence, and content with drug use. This is a comprehensive list of all prohibited topics.

These views and subscriber requirements have been met. To apply for monetization, you can type "YouTube accounts monetization" into Google.

This page will let you start the monetization process. As stated above, you can only view the option to start monetizing after you have met the required requirements.

AdSense Applications

Once your account qualifies for monetization you will see the option of enabling AdSense on videos.

Only accounts in good standing may apply. If your account has not been in good standing, you will receive an email explaining why you weren't accepted into the Partner Program. Do not worry if this happens. You can easily correct the issues highlighted by YouTube'smonetization team and apply again. You can do this by removing the video or editing it that was flagged as inappropriate by YouTube's Monetization team.

After fixing any problems with your account you should be accepted into our Partner Program. You should then be able to add an AdSense account to your channel or create an AdSense new account.

All this is possible on the monetization page.

Is this the right method for you?

YouTube advertising can be simple to set up, although the amount you receive from it is not always predictable. On one month you could make as much revenue as several hundred dollars, while other months you might only get $10.

It's possible to get into this type of earning if you reach the subscriber count and views requirements. To maintain a steady stream of ad income, you'll need to continue to improve your channel. If you are able, upload at most one video per working day.

In reality, this level of productivity can only be achieved if you produce vlogs as well as top 10 lists. It is possible that you won't be able achieve the 1 post per week goal if you are trying to make better videos.

Importantly, you should not create videos longer than 10 minutes. This will limit your ability to maximize your potential income in ad revenues. Your videos can only contain 10 minutes or more ads. This is extremely difficult to accomplish on a daily basis.

Other Monetization Options

YouTube Partner Program has more requirements and views than YouTube, so it is difficult for beginners to monetize their videos using Google Ads.

But don't worry! There are other options. Here are some ways to monetize YouTube videos.

#1 Affiliate Marketing

Affiliate marketing is selling products from other people or businesses online. To become an associate marketer, first apply to an Affiliate Marketing Program of a company, brand, or product you are interested in promoting.

Amazon is the largest affiliate program on English-speaking internet. It is also one among the best beginner affiliate programs. Let's imagine that you own a travel channel. Your travel videos could feature products that you have used. You could also tell your viewers that Amazon Affiliate Link is available in the description for your video if your viewers enjoy the videos.

A commission will be earned if you sell the product to your viewers who click on the affiliate link. This is a way to earn online, even if your channel isn't yet a YouTube partner. Many affiliates earn more from their programs than they do from ad revenue.

Is this the right approach for you?

Affiliate marketing can help you earn a lot. But, affiliate marketing may not be the right way for you to make a living. Comedy channels may not have products to advertise, even though they receive a lot of viewers. This is a way to make money if you make videos with interesting products that your viewers are interested in.

These channels include tutorial channels, review channels, and travel channels.

#2 Video sponsorship

If you have a large number of monthly viewers, companies or individuals might be interested to sponsor your videos. Sponsors will pay you money upfront, before you even create the video. The sponsor will need to then specify how their brand should be presented. Some might say that their brand should be displayed at the beginning and last at least five seconds.

If you and the sponsor agree to the terms of your transaction, you could mention the sponsors in your video according their criteria.

An established YouTube account will help you attract sponsors to invest in the YouTube channel. Your account should have at least 20,000 views each monthly and sufficient videos.

FameBit is a website that will help you check if the channel is suitable for sponsorship. Look for the section titled "Creators".

FameBit allows YouTube creators to meet with potential sponsors through a sort of marketplace called FameBit. FameBit acts as a broker that helps creators find sponsors to support their channel. Creators will need to apply for sponsor programs that are listed on the channel. If they are able to meet the requirements of sponsors, they will be allowed to apply. Your application will then go through. If the creator is accepted, they can begin creating videos to promote their sponsors.

Sponsors may start to look for you as you grow your channel. To make it easier for publishers to reach your channel, ensure that they have a way to contact you.

Is this the right approach for you?

Sponsorship is more effective when you can tackle a niche and have a significant following. Both sports-related channels and fashion bloggers can get sponsorship opportunities. The potential sponsors for fashion bloggers are typically apparel and cosmetic brands.

SeatGeeks and other app developers dominate sponsorship deals for sports channels.

Sponsors in the online learning niche may also be available if you're creating videos about academic subjects. YouTube videos are sometimes sponsored by SkillShare, Udemy, and SkillShare.

Chapter 11: Understanding Youtube Promoted Videos

YouTube is a hugely popular cultural phenomenon and a lot fun. YouTube is part of daily life for millions. YouTube has the potential to make money. We sought out a YouTube partner who could answer our questions about the money to YouTube connection. He shared with us the same advice we have always known: "Making Money is always the tricky bit." The difficult part seems to always be making money. YouTube videos have some great strategies for making money.

First, let me clarify what "making Money" means. Yes, it is possible to make money selling your products or services. YouTube videos can assist with this. It is important to have your name in a positive manner to thousands of people. This will help you brand your business and can also be considered money-making. This is why online video can save you money on customer service, recruiting and other types advertising.

In such a relatively short time, the Internet developed so rapidly. The money generated from online video may seem small at the moment, but it is possible to see how that number could grow exponentially. Video is something we all love. We are able to access more entertainment options, and the Internet offers us more power. If you are looking to make money with online videos, you can still be a leader.

Understanding YouTube Promoted Videos

What exactly is YouTube Promoted Video and how does it work? It's simply an advertisement for a YouTube video. It's a click-to-view ad that is pay-per-click.

PPC Advertising

The dominant form of Internet advertising is pay-per click (PPC). PPC advertising does not charge advertisers for placing the ad. It is cheaper than traditional cost-per million (CPM), where you pay to view or print.

PPC ads have the advantage of being performance-oriented. You don't pay if nobody takes action on your advertisement. This is simple yet powerful.

PPC advertising is paid per-click (CPC). CPC is normally determined by the advertiser's capability to bid on specific keywords. You choose the keyword you want to match with your ad when a user searches that keyword. The search results pages will display your ad.

You can influence how often your ad displays and how high up you are on the search result page. This will affect how high you want to bid for the keyword. Your ad will appear more often if it offers more than the competitors. Your ad will not be seen if it's too cheap (that is, if your offer goes beyond the box).

CPC bids have a bearing on how much you end-up paying. This is because you are competing with other bidders for that keyword. Although you don't have the right to pay the entire bid price, you may only be charged slightly more if you bid higher than your competition. For example, if you are paying $2.00 per Click and $1.00 per Click is the next highest bid you could only be paid $1.10 per Click. In any case, you won't be charged more that the bid amount you specify.

Because only one person clicks on your advertisement will be charged. Even if your advertisement is seen by 100,000 people you only pay for the one click. Your ad may be failing if it only receives one click from 100,000 viewers. How can you predict how many clicks an advertisement will receive in advance? The answer is simple: you are setting aside a pre-budget. YouTube (or any other ad network) will run your ad until it reaches its budget limit. Then, all future shows stop.

Many online ad networks have a daily CPC budget. YouTube included.

You can set a daily spending budget of $100, and then bid $2.00 per click. This will allow your ad to run until you get 50 hits. This would be $100, divided by $2/click. PPC advertising typically links to the top search engines. Google, Yahoo, or Bing are just a few examples. Google AdWords PPC Ad Network is the largest. It places PPC ads directly on Google search results pages. Google also runs PPC advertisements via YouTube if you have an AdWords subscription.

Send viewers to you website

If you want to direct sell a product, it is important to include selling pointers throughout the video. You can think of your video as one the late-night infomercials.

How can you include pointers to sell in your video. Here are some examples of more popular methods:

In the video's title, you can use the URL (or the toll-free telephone number) before. The title card may also contain the product price and any special offers.

Add a credit to your account at the end.

You can overlay the URL of the website or the phone number on the screen throughout the recording.

To create longer images, you can insert a break in center that contains a call for action by an on-screen character such as a PBS pledge.

You can include a simple message of sales in your video script. It's similar to the way infomercial "hosts", inserting their goods into the model.

The bottom line is to not be afraid to talk about the possibility of purchasing the goods. However, it's important that you don't allow the lure of selling to get in the way when presenting the material.

But demand selling with tact.

Alternativly, promote the video by using YouTube's Promoted Video Program. Then, apply a Call to Action Overlay to the clip. You can only sponsor videos with overlays. The overlay allows you to link to your landing pages, where the contract can be concluded.

In the text description of your video, include a sales pitch along with order information. Do not let the viewer re-watch the entire video if he wishes to place an Order.

Close the Sale on Your Site

Now it's time for you to close the deal. The URL that you point to must be a relevant, hard-sell landingpage from your YouTube channel. It is important that the URL you point to not be a generic page or your home page. Both methods require additional customer work.

Instead, link only to the product page of your website. The landing page appears when potential customers click on a link from an advertising platform or search engine. This page should have content. It should be logically linked to the ad. It should include additional information and allow buyers to query them.

You can then create a specific landing page for YouTube videos that is accessible to viewers.

It's as simple as that: You want your customers to be able to give you money as quickly and easily as possible. You should not make potential customers leave your website's home page. They could get lost. They may have trouble finding or giving up on the product they love. You don't want your customers to go to random websites to find the commodity they want. Instead, you want your unique offer to be responded to instantly.

Landing pages help potential clients see the big picture.

You would not get much revenue if someone clicked an ad to buy blenders and found a page bragging on the huge global manufacturing capabilities of your company.

It is easy to convince people to return to your site by using a confusing message.

So that viewers feel the connection, the landing page for your product should reflect the look and feel of the video. If the customer would like to watch the entire recording again, they can include a small clip or even an interactive image. A website should contain more product information than can be seen in a picture.

Some experts suggest a simplified landing page with links to more information for customers. The idea behind this landing page is to convince anyone who visits it to purchase. If they don't buy, then you shouldn't introduce any element that might cause them to reconsider. The click-to order button is, in any case the most important element on the product landing web page. Don't try to make it difficult for customers to order.

Clicking the order button allows the customer to go to either the shopping cart or checkout sections of your website. To track orders, make sure your YouTube video is credited with any orders that flow from the product landing page.

YouTube is a great tool for B2B marketing

YouTube for B2B Advertising: Why?

B2C Marketing is the direct selling of a marketing message to the end consumer. This means that you sell products and services directly to your average retail level customer.

B2B Marketing, on the contrary, communicates a marketing message not to consumers but to other businesses. B2B marketing is different than marketing.

First of all sales ads have less effect on corporations than customers. B2B is more attractive for investors. Businesses are less impulsive in their buying and tend to shop more carefully than consumers. Companies are more likely order directly through suppliers, catalogs or websites. It is also more common to stay with a manufacturer after the purchase cycle is set up.

YouTube is unlikely to help new business customers. YouTube makes it less likely that potential vendors will be found by businesses. Additionally, YouTube users are less likely than others to access YouTube. Many companies prohibit workers from accessing YouTube during company hours. This includes employees in the purchasing section.

YouTube is used for business purposes by many businesses. YouTube estimates that its app searches for 1,5 million companies each day globally. This makes it the second most-used platform for company searching.

YouTube claims that half of online small business owners are served by YouTube; if this is you, YouTube might be the best place to go.

Ways B2B Companies Can Use YouTube

Now that we know YouTube is used by more businesses than ever before, it's time to think about how you can reach them through YouTube. YouTube is primarily a consumer site. This means that the content consumers are most likely to consume won't help a typical business client.

First stuff first. What do B2B YouTube videos should achieve?

B2C marketers focus on attracting new customers through YouTube. I believe this is a lofty goal for B2B marketing. YouTube will not be used by many companies as a source of potential suppliers. Yes, some companies could, but most B2B marketing professionals would be annoyed to search YouTube in search of new contacts. YouTube can be used to offer more information for potential customers and improve existing B2B partnership. It also provides after-sales support. I'll go into detail on each one of these points.

#1 YouTube for additional information

Now that we are aware that YouTube is increasingly used by businesses, the challenge is to figure out how you can reach them via YouTube. YouTube is primarily used as a web-based platform. This means that customers' videos will not be of much use to the average business user.

First of all, stuff. What do you hope to achieve with your B2B YouTube video?

B2C advertisers rely on YouTube to get new customers. B2B marketers are unlikely to achieve that goal. YouTube is unlikely to be the best place for companies to look for suppliers. Yes, some might. However, most B2B marketers would be disgruntled to search YouTube for potential suppliers. YouTube can be used to offer more information to potential customers, improve existing B2B partnership, and provide after-sales service. I will expand on each one of these points.

#2 YouTube for strengthening existing relationships

B2B marketing deals involve the formation and management of partnerships. You are more likely to make additional sales if you have a strong relationship with a customer.

YouTube can be used to build personal relationships that are otherwise inimical. You can give your business a face by creating a video. You can let your company's managers speak directly to customers in videos. Show products in the field, give testimonials from customers... YouTube can be used to interact with your customer base on a regular basis.

#3 Using YouTube for after-sale support

Many B2B products and/or services require high levels post-sales support. You can decrease the need for help by creating a series of how-to videos to address the most common problems.

A series of videos can be made to help clients install equipment. Video tutorials can help you answer common questions about a service you offer. Your professional or customer service representative can help you identify common problems and use your YouTube videos for immediate resolution. Done. You will have satisfied clients and lower support expenses.

Different types B2B videos

YouTube lets you produce and distribute B2B videos that support different goals. Let's start with the most famous.

#1 Product demonstrations and walk throughs

A walk-through or product presentation is beneficial for many reasons. It lets potential customers know more about you and your offerings, which is crucial during decision-making. It also allows customers to discover new products and services.

Product presentations provide valuable information in a quick video format that can be used in any situation. They should be used to support salespeople.

#2 How-To videos

B2B has many uses for step by step videos. Potential clients can benefit from a video on how-to to help them make informed decisions. It could help customers configure and install your products. It can help existing customers make better use of their products and services. Think outside the box. With what you're selling, you can give a lot to your customer base.

#3 Case Studies and Testimonials

A great promotion is to showcase your success stories. Customers love to see the success stories of other customers. For this reason, a video is an excellent forum.

Showcase real-world products, services and get customers to share their love for what you do.

#4 Conventions, Events

YouTube can be used by your organization to promote these events and provide information while it hosts or organizes workshops, conventions, and other special events. Make a teaser reel to get people interested in attending a future event. Or record the event and upload it (or a few highlights) online.

You would be surprised how many viewers you could attract -- including potential new customers--especially if you have well-known or interesting presenters. YouTube can also be used for internal sales conferencing videos.

These cases might be attractive to customers. In any case, you can gain more leverage by making them available for possible streaming.

#5 Business Notes, Video Blogs

The management update audio is the talking head picture of the president or chief executive of your organization speaking directly to your client base. These videos are not my favorites, but if the CEO has a great presence, business influence, and a proven partnership relationship with your customers, this strategy will help you improve existing connections or make new ones.

This form is not just for upper management.

You can have a video blog, which is a way for employees at all levels of your company to discuss industry trends and product development. It is safe to say that selling to other businesses will be easier if you work with people who are deeply involved in their business and other topics. Provide knowledge, advice and an opinion-filled vlog to satisfy the customer's hunger. You'd be amazed at how many potential customers will take just two to three minutes for you to explain your ideas.

YouTube's Best Practices for B2B Advertising

YouTube for B2B Marketing has some best practices. While many of these practices are the same as those used by B2C advertisers they are worth repeating.

Chapter 12: How To Get Youtube Monetization Started

* Click the YouTube link to earn money.

* In the top-right corner, click the symbol to signify your account. Then, choose YouTube Studio.

* Select Monetization under Other Features from the left-hand side menu

* Read the Partner Program Terms and click on I Agree.

* Create an AdSense new account for your channel.

* Set your preferences regarding monetization.

* Click the Return button to return to the Dashboard and select Analytics.

* Click on Revenue in top-left corner. Then scroll down until the Monthly Estimated Sales chart appears. This graphic will give you an indication of your expected monthly income.

YouTube Monetization: How Many Views Are Required?

YouTube views and profits do not directly correlate. While you might get thousands upon thousands of views, it doesn't mean that anyone clicks on your ads.

YouTube also has specific requirements regarding the payment of publishers who run ads on their channels. A viewer must click the advertisement or watch the entire video in order to receive money.

But there's good news for YouTube marketers who want to learn how to monetize YouTube. You don't have solely to rely on ads to generate income. YouTube Premium may allow you to make money without clicking or watching ads.

How to Buy A YouTube Premium Feature

YouTube Premium is the only way to make money. YouTube Premium is the answer.

YouTube Premium makes it possible for users to enjoy videos without ads interrupting their viewing. YouTube Premium subscribers will see the creators' videos and automatically generate another revenue stream. Creators don't need to do any extra.

In accordance with YouTube's rules for monetizing profits through advertising, the majority revenue generated from Premium memberships will go to creators. (Total revenue distribution depends on how many Premium users watch your content).

Premium subscribers will also be able download their videos, watch them offline, and even play them in the background. This will increase their viewing time.

Promoting Channel Memberships

Channel memberships are a great way to increase your YouTube channel's revenue. A $4.99/month membership plan is available to fans. It offers benefits like early access, exclusive emojis and live chat for members. Members will be identified by special badges only for them in comments, livechat, and the Community tab.

Channel memberships make perfect sense, as viewers know how difficult it can be for YouTube creators to pay attention. There you have it, another strategy for monetizing YouTube channels.

You can encourage your visitors to become members by using your videos.

Add Affiliate Products Endorsements to Your Videos

YouTube channels are an excellent way to increase your business's visibility.

Once you have established a significant following on the website, companies will likely start contacting your and asking for you to market their products in return. Sign up to become an affiliate and use product placement in the videos. Affiliate programs are a great way to grow your network.

While it may be a great way of making extra income, you should exercise caution as the viewers are likely to know when anything is being bought.

YouTube regulations require that you only promote products that your audience finds useful. If you do, you should inform your viewers of any partnerships.

Super Chat Can Be Used To Monetize Livestreams

Super Chat is a very popular YouTube revenue stream. This tool allows viewers the ability to buy chat comments that standout and even place them at the top in a stream's comments. Super Chat allows you to monetize live streams on YouTube.

Super Chat gets 30% of the YouTube monetization rate earnings, which range from $1-500. To organize and market live streams, it is essential that everyone asks how to earn money through YouTube Superchat.

Promote them in videos, and on other social media sites.

Get YouTube Influencer Status

Creatives have the opportunity to become part of the growing influencer marketing market.

But where to begin? YouTube marketing guru and influencer suggested artists to calculate a flat-rate by multiplying their videos' normal amount of views by 15% per view.

The following figures show how much YouTube Influencers can expect to make in the future:

* $20,000 per video for creators with over a million subscribers

* $12,000 per video for creatives with 100,000 subscribers

* 200 per video for creatives with 10,000 followers

It will be easier to get more by partnering with companies whose products you value.

These influencer marketplaces will help you to be seen by potential business partners.

Channel Pages: Join forces with businesses and other YouTubers

Grapevine Logic requires only 1,000 followers to join.

While you may find influencer networks that connect you with businesses looking to pay top-dollar, others could offer free goods. Consider the best options for you.

Motivate people to buy your products

You can promote your products on YouTube. It's a great way of driving more traffic to you website and promoting the products in your videos.

Shopify makes opening a store easy if it hasn't been done before. Once your store has been set up, you can sell whatever products or items you think your audience might like. If you're looking at ways to make YouTube more profitable, this is a great option.

How to Earn Money With YouTube Videos

If you want to make YouTube videos that generate revenue, here are some things you need to be aware of.

Make your videos at least 10 minutes long

YouTube videos of more than 10 minute duration increase your chances to make more money with commercials. YouTube videos of longer duration are more viewable than

YouTube videos of less than 10 minute length. This is beneficial for the amount of ad dollars these videos could bring in. YouTube's search results will rank longer-viewed videos higher, which will increase your chances of getting visitors to view your material.

Join forces with YouTubers

One strategy to monetize videos on YouTube is to collaborate with other YouTubers. This great technique will help you grow your YouTube audience, add original content to your channel, as well as make your content easily accessible to a wide audience. Look up YouTubers who are popular in your niche. Then, get in touch and share your brilliant idea with them.

Produce educational and engaging content

Your YouTube channel's success is dependent on this. YouTube users are constantly searching for entertainment and useful content. You can make your audience more likely to view all of the video content and return for more.

Pro Tip: Take a look at your YouTube stats in order to determine which demographic is most likely to be watching your videos. This will help you get a better picture of the content that you should produce. Consider including some of Gen Z's preferred slang terms in your films, for instance, if you notice that Gen Z viewers enjoy them.

Maximize Detail Descriptions

Descriptions are another great way to make money from YouTube videos. They aid viewers in finding your material, and making a decision about whether to view it or not. The best advice for journalistic writing is to start with the most important details, and work your way down from there. Also, make sure to highlight the benefits viewers get by watching the entire movie. Finally, be sure to speak in a manner that your audience can understand.

Increase your following by posting often

It is a great idea to manage a YouTube channel with consistent content posting. Your viewers will remain interested in your channel if there is a steady stream content. Your viewers will become more aware of the internet presence you have and any assets related to it, including your e-commerce business.

How to Make YouTube Videos Without Being Paid

It is possible to monetize YouTube without making your videos. However, you can reuse the work of others. YouTube offers a wide variety of licensed videos under Creative Commons.

You can publish or monetize videos by other people under certain license types. You can, for example, use a film you found under the CC BY license and make modifications to it.

How can I make money using YouTube?

YouTube users may be interested in learning how to make money from the platform. You will need to establish a few things in order for the business to be paid.

First, you will need to create a Google AdSense profile with your Gmail ID. Next, choose your preferred payment option from wire transfers and Western Union QuickCash to EFT, EFT, or cheques.

If you are located in a tax-exempt area, you may be asked about your tax details while creating an AdSense account. After AdSense is set up, once you have reached the minimum payment level, payment can be requested. Google won't allow you to choose the form of payment until your earnings reach the amount shown in your local currency. Google doesn't issue payments for amounts lower than these levels.

How to Make Money on YouTube Despite All the Competition

As you are learning how to monetize your YouTube channel remember that there will also be other business owners competing for viewers. You'll also find professional YouTubers competing with you for your audience's attention.

This is an important point to remember when you are creating content for your channel. Video thumbnails and titles can help you stand out among the rest. YouTube is a visually-focused medium. It's important that you do things correctly to increase the number of people who view your videos.

Your success can be greatly affected by the quality of the audio and videos in your content. To present your brand as an expert and professional, you need high-quality video content.

YouTube SEO can be used to your advantage to surpass the competition. To increase organic traffic to YouTube, you can create SEO material to describe your videos.

YouTube SEO 101: How to create a YouTube Keyword Strategy

You aren't the only one who has ever considered creating videos for your business, but decided to put it off because it seemed so chaotic.

Many business owners are hesitant to make videos because of the initial cost. YouTube videos, in particular, are less expensive than traditional methods to reach your target market.

Jumpshot, Alexa and Google say YouTube is the 2nd most popular website worldwide and the 2nd-largest international search engine. A brand could benefit tremendously from this. Is it possible to present yourself to your target markets while they are actively looking for your products and services? Please, yes.

Search engine optimization (SEO), which is a strategy that optimizes videos for YouTube, will help you to maximize the ROI of your investment.

By planning for SEO right from the start, you'll be providing the content people want. This allows you to attract relevant traffic for months, or even years. An SEO-friendly YouTube video that performs well in search results is a valuable resource that will eventually pay off.

To maximize your limited time, plan for SEO friendly YouTube videos. Your efforts will not vanish in one day, or drop to the bottom in your social media feeds within a few weeks.

However, to reach that goal you will need to master the basics of optimizing and organizing your YouTube videos. Here is how to do this.

YouTube Content Planning 101

It is essential to include your videos in your overall content plan for your company before you start optimizing them.

A few key points will help you determine if it is worth producing films for your company.

You need a plan for how and what you are going to create it.

Recognize Your Audience

The first step in creating your strategy is to understand your target market. YouTube's goal is to help you find the content that you are searching for.

Take a look at your ideal customer and how they relate to you brand. Does your product fulfill their needs? Are people supporting you because they are emotionally connected with you or because you have a great brand? These questions can help guide you in your choice of video content.

Choose a type Of Video

It doesn't matter if talking to the camera makes you uncomfortable. And expensive, high-tech equipment may not be necessary. Screen-sharing movies can be taken of you walking through a slideshow presentation from your PC. You can also record excellent video with your phone's camera.

The only thing that limits your possibilities is your imagination. Your path is clear if you choose the video format that best engages your audience.

But, how can we choose the right content for our audience? The key is to know your audience and to produce material that informs and entertains. You can create a buyer persona to help you identify your ideal customer if this is not already done.

Develop A Keyword Strategy

A keyword strategy is key to a successful YouTube channel. It will help to produce content that users like and can rank well in searches. These are two key elements that will ensure your video marketing efforts succeed.

You should be able use the basic content strategy that was created to outline what you want and how to achieve it. Now, it is time to dissect your strategy into potential themes and keyphrases for the channel. After you have chosen a topic to focus on, such as "dog training", or "styling scarves", you can begin to test the phrases and terms that customers will use to search for answers.

A keyword strategy will be the cornerstone for a YouTube channel.

You can keep track of your ideas as you look for keywords. Keep it simple and include:

You can choose the exact keyword you would like to appear in search results.

Search Activity: This indicates the average monthly number searches for that keyword.

Keyword Competition: This indicates the number ads that use that keyword. It is a proxy, however, organic competition cannot always be accurately measured using this metric.

Analyzing keywords

Chrome extension Keywords Everywhere, and Firefox plugin Keywords Everywhere make it easy to do keyword research on YouTube. Simply type in the phrase or word that you are interested targeting in the search field. Keywords Everywhere can show you the monthly searches volume, keyword difficulty, as well cost per Click for advertising.

Also, all data related to any suggested searches will be displayed. This can help you discover a term that you haven't considered before.

TubeBuddy, a browser plugin with both paid and free tiers that allows you to perform keyword analysis, is another tool. TubeBuddy will automatically display keyword analysis in the sidebar.

TubeBuddy will let you know if the keyword is a combination of search volume or competitiveness. This information can be used to guide your strategy and not just for you to interpret.

No matter which tool you use, search for keywords that are balanced in search volume and competition. This will depend on your target market and industry. It is possible to find lower volume keywords that have a higher conversion. This could be because the keywords receive more traffic, but they are more likely make a sale. Learning from the beginning is the best way to discover what works and how to improve your knowledge.

Competitive Analysis

To broaden or develop your keyword strategy, you can also conduct competitive research. YouTube will always have at minimum a few channels that produce content similar to what your target audience is looking for, even if those channels aren't your direct competitors.

* Select a few channels in your market that are successful. Now, you can use their success as a guide for your own.

* Check out which videos have the most views.

* To view videos from each competitor's YouTube channel, click the "Videos" tab.

* By default, the tab's top will display the most recent uploads. Select "Sortby..." to arrange it so your most watched videos appear at the top.

* This can be a great way to help you think of new topics that may be relevant to your clients.

Explore the Popular Tags in Video

You can get a good idea of which formats and content work best for your keyword by looking at the videos in the top position for keywords. TubeBuddy lets you peek at what TubeBuddy does behind the scenes. It allows you to see which tags were used for the best-performing videos.

You might sell hijabs and your clients might be interested to know more about the different styling options. TubeBuddy will allow you to view the tags in the top-ranking TubeBuddy video for "wedding hijab lesson" at the side of the video.

These tags are useful for both keyword suggestions and guidance in determining the tags you should use on your films.

Searchability Optimization for Your Content

Once you have determined which keyword should be the focus of your video's content, it's now time to optimize it so YouTube can recognize that your video is a good fit.

It's something we will return to many times. But it's worth noting that your primary goal in SEO should be to help YouTube understand your content. It's not difficult. But what really matters is that your content is clear and consistent for your audience to find what they want.

YouTube should be able to understand the subject matter in your material, and then optimize it.

Title

SEO is two-fold: your video title and your meta description.

Click-Through Rate Impacted by Search Terms: People who search for your term will not only find your videos, but they will also see a list related results. Your title must grab their attention and persuade to click.

YouTube will recognize if your video matches the term well if people click on it more than other titles.

YouTube recognizes keywords. Because YouTube needs to know your title in order to determine how relevant your video can be to a particular keyword, it will include your main keyword.

You should stay clear of clickbait. You should avoid using exaggerated words or punctuation. YouTube clearly states that clickbait, even if not in direct contradiction to their community guidelines will not perform well when searching.

Thumbnails

You can have greater control over what viewers see because a thumbnail is displayed alongside your YouTube search result. Optimizing thumbnails can improve your click-through and watchtime. You can also include additional information about the video, such as what viewers can anticipate.

You may also submit creative photos to your video's thumbnail. YouTube says custom thumbnails are found on 90% of the most popular videos.

It's important to include your title in your thumbnail. Both of these factors can have an effect on your click through rate.

Your thumbnail should be captivating and accurately represent the video. It may get you a lot of clicks, but people might leave almost immediately if it is confusing. YouTube shows clearly that this action will reduce your video's visibility on search results.

YouTube claims that your thumbnail, like your title, is another important piece of metadata. To maximize the use of your image file, include your keyword in the filename. Let people know that your video has a keyword-related title is another approach.

One last point to remember: YouTube suggests that your thumbnail images adhere to the suggested ratio and size of YouTube thumbnails. These are 1280pxx796px. Thumbnails should be at least 640px wide.

Description

In the description of your film, you can use your main keyword to repeat and include as much relevant information as possible. You can use 5,000 characters to describe your film. There are however specific rules you must follow.

Your Major Keywords should be used early in your career

YouTube advises you to use your keyword as soon as possible in your description. This can help people identify if they have found what they need and should view your video. YouTube will also see this as an indicator that your video does indeed contain that keyword.

Pay attention to the first and second sentences

YouTube allows you to use 5,000 characters. But, that would make it difficult to read every word in every video. Experts believe that the 100 first characters are the most important. However, this number will depend on where your video is being broadcast.

Accordingly, the video's title and the first line of the description, as well as the first sentence, are important pieces of content. Your keyword should be included and made compelling.

Learn to compose in every day language

While it can be tempting for you to stuff your description full of keywords, the best way that users will see your videos and help them rank higher is to provide a simple description that accurately describes what the video is about. YouTube recommends that you do not list your keywords in your description because tags are meant to be used for tagging.

Create a default description of each video that covers the essentials

It's possible to make that information the channel's default description, if you regularly add the same store descriptions, social media

links, and product page URL links to each video.
).

In the sidebar of your Creator Studio, choose "Channel", to change your default description. This section is where you can manage YouTube and your videos. Next, select "Upload defaults".

You have the option to choose from several settings for each video submitted, but the main one that you need to pay attention to is the description. It is a great method to save time, as the default description will automatically be added at the end of each description you upload.

Tags

YouTube can help you with the tags. Consider your tags as a collection or terms you wish YouTube to recognize for your video.

YouTube says that adding pointless tags will not benefit you long-term. YouTube recommends not using trendy words or phrases to improve your video's visibility. Be sure to use tags that are relevant to your actual video content.

Time Observed

YouTube appreciates that users are loyal. YouTube views are one of their main measures. If you can keep YouTube users watching your films for longer periods of time, they will be more satisfied. They've made it clear that search results are influenced by watch time.

This could seem counterintuitive to companies. Although you want to rank well on YouTube, your customers should be able to visit your store to make a purchase. You will eventually find the important word.

These four strategies can help you make the most of your time with television.

* Make a Script for Your Video. You will be able to convey your arguments more succinctly, and your viewers will be more interested in your videos if you have a written script.

* Play Cards - If you have relevant content, especially YouTube videos, you can link directly to it in a play card that appears as your visitors watch.

* Use End Screens These screens are a great way to direct viewers toward other films on your channel.

* Set up Playlists - This allows viewers to automatically play the next video when they have finished the current one. A carefully planned playlist can help you keep viewer engagement with relevant content.

You should remember that the number of views a video has affects its rank in search results. So optimizing your content is your top priority. If your viewers are enticed to watch more of your content, they will be more likely to subscribe to YouTube and become customers.

User interaction

YouTube also uses engagement metrics, which are a ranking factor in search, and watch time. There you will see your subscribers, comments, favorite, and favorites. Asking viewers for their "likes, comments, and subscriptions!" This is partly what motivates this. YouTube video scripting is a complex business.

We ask that you "like, comment, or subscribe" because of this.

While it may seem clichéd, the "" plays a major role in YouTube scripting.

To increase these numbers, you can treat your YouTube comment section like a critical space for engaging your customers. Respond quickly to any comments that you receive. People who know you read and respond more often are more likely than others to comment on your next videos.

Transcripts and Captions

Although transcripts in your videos can make your content easier to understand and help increase watch time for those who don't want sound, how does it affect your video's SEO?

While it's unclear if uploading custom transcriptions is associated with higher search ranking, it is important to not ignore it. YouTube is able to understand more of your video by adding more text. Google has indicated a preference to include accessibility features in search results.

Facebook Shares

Google clearly states that social media shares do not impact search engine results. YouTube is different.

One study has shown that YouTube videos with more social media shares are associated with better search results.

YouTube can track more videos and this makes it easier to manipulate. YouTube hasn't stated explicitly that social share affects search engine result. However, YouTube's metrics that include social media data and high correlation lead to the conclusion, that the more socially shared videos, the better their SEO.

Optimize Your Videos to Get the Best Out of Them

YouTube is an excellent way to differentiate yourself from your competitors. YouTube's video creation process is not for everyone. It requires more work up front so many companies don't invest as heavily in the video.

Optimizing your keywords for keywords people are already searching can help you maximize your investment. Optimizing your videos for YouTube to be found when users search for particular keywords is crucial. It's the best way to ensure your videos continue to bring in revenue long after they are published.

Chapter 13: Youtube's Algorithm Operates

Many video producers see the YouTube algorithm, which is used by professional YouTubers and companies to increase their views, as a higher power. It is totally beyond their control.

They say that YouTube's algorithm is hard to understand. It's one the platform's most well-kept secrets.

But it is not.

A group of Google engineers presented their ideas on how YouTube should display videos through its recommendation system to improve user experiences in a research paper that was published in 2016.

YouTube's product managers made a video explaining to users that YouTube's recommendation system was designed to help them find the right content to enjoy long-term pleasure.

YouTube SEO, Social Media Marketing, and Obtaining Subscribers are all frequently mentioned in connection to increasing YouTube's views. YouTube's recommendation systems (through the YouTube homepage or "recommended For You" suggestions) do not provide unlimited views. They help people find your videos, but they are not the most effective way to get them.

YouTube Algorithm. What is it?

YouTube algorithm is a collection of computer instructions used to process videos, related content, comments, descriptions and engagements. The algorithms help to rank and suggest videos based on relevancy and audience enjoyment.

What Does YouTube's Algorithm Look Like in 2022

YouTube's algorithm was designed to make it as easy and straightforward as possible for people to find the best content. YouTube's main objective is to encourage users to keep watching videos and increase customer retention.

YouTube's algorithm began as a result of users clicking through videos. This led to clickbait headlines, which sometimes left viewers unsatisfied by the video's true content.

It began shifting towards timing in 2012 when it was more favorable. Based on how often viewers watched certain channels or movies, suggestions videos were displayed. That was how it remained for approximately three years until YouTube came up with a better alternative.

YouTube has seen a significant improvement in audience enjoyment since 2015. Since 2015, YouTube has been a better place for users to enjoy.

YouTube Does It Assess User Satisfaction?

* It sends millions to people each month with surveys asking for feedback. But, they probably only see about two to three.

* It notifies viewers when they use the "Not interest" option to watch videos.

* It looks at the shares, likes, and dislikes of a video.

* The following signals have been broken down by Google engineers. They are used by YouTube to rank films and make recommendations.

* Rates for click-through (the probability of someone clicking on your video once they've seen it)

* Watch time (the sum of the time viewers spend watching your videos together)

* How many videos of your channel have the users viewed?

* How many times has the viewer viewed the video?

* What have you already searched for?

* The user has viewed past videos

* Geographical and demographic data for the user

* The three first signals are the only ones that you can directly influence.

* The rest of the elements will be influenced by variables beyond your channel.

They state that their ultimate ranking goal consists of "often a simple function of projected viewing length per impression." Ranking based upon click-through rate often promotes misleading films that users never finish, a practice called "clickbait", but watch time accurately reflects engagement.

Although some people might think this means YouTube would punish you if your optimization for click-throughs is not true, it is a common misconception.

Only bait-and-switch strategies--overpromising before the click and offering subpar content after it--are penalized by YouTube. The click through rate is still vital today. Without clicks, it's impossible to get a lot more YouTube watch time.

These priorities can also be seen in YouTube Studio when you look at your YouTube statistics dashboard.

Below the Reach Viewers page you may find the following stats, which together demonstrate YouTube's new focus upon click-through rate (and watch time):

Impressions: The number and frequency with which visitors view the thumbnails of your videos (as suggested videos) on the homepage or in search result results.

YouTube was the place where your video thumbnails were displayed for potential viewers.

Click-Through Ratio (CTR for Impressions): The number of times your thumbnails viewers viewed a given video. This is based on log in impressions.

Views Following Impressions - The frequency with which people watched your films after a YouTube discovery.

Time from impressions: Check out the time generated by YouTube users that viewed and clicked your videos.

How YouTube sets up the algorithm

YouTube users will see most recommended videos on YouTube's homepage. They also see them when they view other videos. YouTube uses a different algorithm for these recommendations.

Let's now discuss why certain videos appear at each site.

Homepage

From the moment you launch the YouTube mobile app or access YouTube.com, you will arrive at the homepage. YouTube is determined to draw users in and keep them using the app for as long time as possible.

There are two criteria that will be used to assess homepage videos.

Performance of the Video

Personalization: Your specific viewing preferences and viewing history.

YouTube does not know what motivates a viewer to visit YouTube. YouTube must therefore rely only on what it does know, which is based in part on what viewers have seen.

Recommended Video

You'll find the recommended videos section in the right-hand sidebar, just below the video you're currently watching (or directly above it if your mobile app is being used).

These videos are suggested by the algorithm based what you most likely to see next. It is also based your viewing history for this session. These criteria include:

* Videos that are most often seen in groups

* Videos about related subjects

* Videos you've previously viewed

YouTube can show you more videos tailored to your current session, rather than showing you a wide selection of videos it believes you might enjoy. YouTube also knows why you're visiting YouTube's site at this particular time.

7 Methods to Expand Your YouTube Account

1. You should stick to a consistent format or idea for your YouTube channel.

A majority of YouTube channels and series can be summarized in five seconds.

A lot of YouTube channels and content creators find it difficult to grow their followings, as they use the channel more as a place for all their video content rather than as a place where they can host a regular series.

YouTube success is built upon consistency.

YouTube creators who maintain consistency are able expand their viewership and subscribers because users will be more likely to choose to see more of the content they have and subscribe to their channel.

Celebrities enjoying food is a popular theme on The First We Feast channel. It features several episodes that are almost variations of the same theme.

The consistency of the content and stickiness of its premise give viral videos a better chance at turning every viewer into a loyal member.

It is a good idea to make any deviations from the main point of your YouTube account so that you don't lose your effort. First We Feast is owned and operated by Complex, a website which has a different purpose and readership. The Featured channel tab links the channels together. However, they don't cross paths.

There may be a free video editor that lets you upload your videos in one click. You can publish movies fast and without the need for downloading or uploading files.

2. Add More Sources to The Recommendation Machine

The recommendation system can't be relied on to drive all views to YouTube channels.

Recommendations rely on how your viewers have engaged with your content. YouTube would be without the information it needs to base its recommendations if people didn't see your videos. All the usual methods are available to promote your videos.

* Sending new videos and information to your email subscribers

* Collaborating and collaborating with media outlets, influencers, etc.

* Promoting your video content through social media

* Launching an affiliate campaign on YouTube

YouTube SEO and growing subscribers are key factors YouTube algorithms considers when making personalized suggestions. This will help increase video views over the long-term.

The study by engineers revealed that the "essential signals" indicate previous interactions with the item as well other related products. For instance, take the user's past interactions with this channel. How many videos has the user viewed from this channel? What date did the user watch the most recent video on this subject in its entirety?

This will increase the chance that you videos will be shown to new users when they next open YouTube. You can encourage them to continue watching your films after they click through.

3. Produce Clickable Thumbnails

We have demonstrated that click-throughs are still vital and that YouTube giving watch priority is a defense mechanism to stop clickbait with poor quality.

Let's discuss how to increase your click through rate using two fantastic resources for creating clickable thumbnails, Netflix and YouTube's Trending Videos Page.

Do action shots of expressive faces or close-ups

YouTube's video thumbnails feature many animated and emotive faces.

Netflix performed an analysis of the artwork that was uploaded to its platform and found that emotions were a good way to convey subtle details. The human brain is programmed to react to faces. This can be seen across all media. It's important to remember that faces displaying nuanced emotions are more effective than ones with neutral or stoic emotions.

Netflix observed a first pattern in thumbnails. A thumbnail's propensity is to outperform all others when it has three or more people.

Your thumbnails should include at least one face with expressions that speak volumes to increase click-throughs.

If you don't have expressive faces in your videos, you can evoke strong feelings by using action-packed thumbnails.

The rule of thirds is a good rule to follow when creating your thumbnail.

The rule to thirds might be able to provide a more simple way to get the "golden rate," which can reduce the processing time of our brains for images.

The rule of image composition dictates that you place your point or interest in the first or third of the frame and not the middle.

You can use your thumbnail to grab the attention of the viewer to the most important information in your image. But it's more a suggestion than a definitive rule.

Give Your Thumbnails A Text

According to a professional 2019, YouTube now accounts 37% of all mobile web traffic. You can also expect some users to access your videos via their mobile devices.

Because it is prominent in relation to your title, the user's eyes are almost certain to be drawn to your thumbnail. If they find your visual interesting enough, they will be more inclined to read the headline and click the link.

Therefore, why not include language in the thumbnail? This will aid readers in making a choice.

Your video's title can be used as the text, or perhaps just a few lines to describe its hook. You should ensure that your thumbnails convey the content of your video. This is true even if your visitors only use thumbnails to read on mobile devices.

Personalize your thumbnails

If you check out the trending tab you will see that many trending YouTube videos have optimized their first impression using the strategies we discussed above.

Make it easy for viewers of your videos to identify them at a glance. This will increase the likelihood that they will get clicked on by those who are already familiarized with your content.

If you want to brand your thumbnails, make sure that your YouTube channel has a standard layout. This will allow them to stand out from other recommended videos.

4. At Click, Motivate Visitors to Stay.

It's easy to get viewers to your videos. Another way is to get viewers to watch your entire video.

You can increase the rate at which your videos are completed and get more views by including this goal during your video creation process.

* Make sure to start strong with your introduction.

* Watch your videos quietly by transcribing.

* Adjust the length of your videos in line with your analytics (how much time users spend watching before stopping)).

Avoid repeating shots too often or you will bore your audience. (This is why jump cuts on YouTube are so popular).

* In order to keep the viewer's interest refocused when your video becomes too long, you can intersperse it by using short breaks.

* Request that viewers subscribe to your videos. Click the Subscribe button. Or, you can watch other videos at each end screen.

5. Promote Marathon Viewing on Your Channel

You can optimize the watch time of a channel by using methods that include watching videos repeatedly.

Here are some ways that viewers may be motivated to watch more content from your YouTube channel.

* Manually recommending related videos via cards or end cards

* Linking to playlists for videos whenever you share. This will ensure that your video appears next to the user.

* Use a consistent format from the thumbnail to your actual video. This will help viewers anticipate how they will like your other videos.

* Use clips from other films or calls to action to direct viewers to see more content

* Cards are a great way to help your viewers explore the rabbit hole of your YouTube channel. It is also smart to enable subtitles in all of your videos. This allows viewers to keep watching, even if they are not hearing the sound.

6. Make your Content Keyword-Optimized

YouTube is a search tool, so optimizing YouTube videos for a specific keyword and a few other keywords can make them more visible on YouTube search results. The algorithm will also be able to better understand your content and recommend it at the right time.

It is important to first do keyword research on the platform in order to identify which video themes or keywords are popular and may appeal to your target audience. TubeBuddy Chrome plug-in can help you identify the most relevant keywords.

Enter your keyword in the search box and then check out TubeBuddy's statistics at the sidebar. Before you search for the perfect keyword, it is worth trying several others.

Search for keywords with an overall score of "Very good" or "Excellent". But if your YouTube videos receive consistently high rankings, you can often ignore the "Competition". This is because your channel has already been a strong rival.

You'll need to ensure that the keywords are included in the video's title description and tags. You may also want to include some hashtags at the bottom for organization of your video content.

7. Pay attention to your YouTube competitors

Are there YouTube rivals to you? Do you know of any YouTube competitors? If so, be aware of the types and content they are putting out. Remember that you want your video recommended over theirs.

Pay close attention to such details as:

* Most popular videos

* No matter what episodes or playlists are produced

* How involved is their audience

* How they create their metadata, titles and descriptions of videos

You can build trust with your viewers by covering the same topics as your competition. It will also help you to focus your strategy.

One thing will always be the same, despite all the changes made to YouTube's algorithm.

YouTube's algorithm was subject to many changes over the years. Businesses and creators are left puzzled by why their strategies don't work anymore.

Even though YouTube's algorithm may change, the goal of the platform is to increase interaction and viewers with YouTube videos. You are not dissimilar to their goals.

Chapter 14: How To Market On Youtube: An Introduction

We live in the video age.

YouTube and technology, as well as the internet, have given people greater access than media companies. According to 73 per cent of consumers, videos influence their shopping decisions. Videos are the most popular kind of material consumers can view from social media companies.

YouTube is the multiplier in your video marketing strategy. It's possible to achieve things that you never thought possible if it is done correctly.

This guide will teach you how to promote yourself on YouTube with case studies from successful YouTube producers and companies.

YouTube: A successful marketing tool

The answer is yes. YouTube marketing is the best way for your business to reach its audience.

YouTube is the second most popular website worldwide. YouTube boasts a global audience, with 42.9 per cent of the internet's total population viewing it each month. YouTube is used to host more than one million hours of content each day.

YouTube users account for more than 2.3 Billion monthly users. It's likely that your target audience visits YouTube at least occasionally if they are online.

YouTube might be thought to be only for big brands with millions upon millions of viewers. YouTube is an extremely powerful platform and small companies can gain market share. YouTube ads have doubled in number over the past 2 years.

YouTube videos that show your products and review your brand can be a powerful tool to increase your sales.

www.ingramcontent.com/pod-product-compliance
Lightning Source LLC
Chambersburg PA
CBHW050412120526
44590CB00015B/1931